RESEARCH MEMORANDUM ON INTERNAL MIGRATION IN THE DEPRESSION

By WARREN S. THOMPSON

ARNO PRESS

A NEW YORK TIMES COMPANY

Reprint Edition 1972 by Arno Press Inc.

Reprinted from a copy in The Newark Public Library

LC# 70-162840
ISBN 0-405-00843-0

Studies in the Social Aspects of the Depression
ISBN for complete set: 0-405-00840-6
See last pages of this volume for titles.

Manufactured in the United States of America

STUDIES

IN THE

SOCIAL ASPECTS

OF THE

DEPRESSION

Studies in the Social Aspects of the Depression

Advisory Editor: *ALEX BASKIN*

State University of New York at Stony Brook

Preface to the New Edition

THE IMAGE OF AN OLD FLIVVER packed with sullen-faced people, broken mattresses and other battered belongings has been imprinted on the American mind through the stark photographs of Dorothea Lange and Walker Evans. The problem of people adrift on the land was very real in the 1930's. Dust storms and soil erosion, drought and soil exhaustion—all worked to make transients of families whose forebears had lived on the land for generations. Migration led to rural depopulation in some areas and to family disorganization in general. Young boys and girls, hoping to ease the burdens of their parents, took to the road and the rails. In the cities, unemployed industrial workers, numbed by endless waiting in employment and bread lines, took to the open road as an avenue of escape and hope. They abandoned the grey metropolis in search of the future and a decent life. Warren Thompson's study probes the problems which grew out of this mass internal migration in the United States. He examined the diverse and complex series of events which took families off the land and out of the cities and put them in motion on the highways. He surveyed the theories and described the studies which sought to explain this unusual phenomenon in twentieth-century America. In an era when hobos, drifters and bindle stiffs have been replaced by a new generation of wanderers and seekers, it is surprising to discover that many of the same forces and questions are pertinent today.

Alex Baskin
Stony Brook, New York, 1971

BULLETIN 30

1937

RESEARCH MEMORANDUM ON INTERNAL MIGRATION IN THE DEPRESSION

By WARREN S. THOMPSON
Scripps Foundation
Miami University

PREPARED UNDER THE DIRECTION OF THE
COMMITTEE ON STUDIES IN SOCIAL
ASPECTS OF THE DEPRESSION

SOCIAL SCIENCE RESEARCH COUNCIL
230 PARK AVENUE   NEW YORK NY

The Social Science Research Council was organized in 1923 and formally incorporated in 1924, composed of representatives chosen from the seven constituent societies and from time to time from related disciplines such as law, geography, psychiatry, medicine, and others. It is the purpose of the Council to plan, foster, promote, and develop research in the social field.

CONSTITUENT ORGANIZATIONS

American Anthropological Association

American Economic Association

American Historical Association

American Political Science Association

American Psychological Association

American Sociological Society

American Statistical Association

FOREWORD

By the Committee on Studies in
Social Aspects of the Depression

THIS monograph on research pertaining to internal migration in the depression is one of a series of thirteen sponsored by the Social Science Research Council to stimulate the study of depression effects on various social institutions. The full list of titles is on page ii.

The depression of the early 1930's was like the explosion of a bomb dropped in the midst of society. All the major social institutions, such as the government, family, church, and school, obviously were profoundly affected and the repercussions were so far reaching that scarcely any type of human activity was untouched. The facts about the impact of the depression on social life, however, have been only partially recorded. It would be valuable to have assembled the vast record of influence of this economic depression on society. Such a record would constitute an especially important preparation for meeting the shock of the next depression, if and when it comes. Theories must be discussed and explored now, if much of the information to test them is not to be lost amid ephemeral sources.

The field is so broad that selection has been necessary. In keeping with its mandate from the Social Science Research Council, the Committee sponsored no studies of an exclusively economic or political nature. The subjects chosen for inclusion were limited in number by resources. The final selection was made by the Committee from a larger number of proposed subjects, on the basis of social importance and available personnel.

Although the monographs clearly reveal a uniformity of goal, they differ in the manner in which the various authors sought to attain that goal. This is a consequence of the Committee's belief that the promotion of research could best be served by not imposing rigid restrictions on the organization of materials by the contributors. It is felt that the encouraged freedom in approach and organization has resulted in the enrichment of the individual reports and of the series as a whole.

A common goal without rigidity in procedure was secured by requesting each author to examine critically the literature on the depression for the purpose of locating existing data and interpretations already reasonably well established, of discovering the more serious inadequacies in information, and of formulating research problems feasible for study. He was not expected to do this research himself. Nor was he expected to compile a full and systematically treated record of the depression as experienced in his field. Nevertheless, in indicating the new research which is needed, the writers found it necessary to report to some extent on what is known. These volumes actually contain much information on the social influences of the depression, in addition to their analyses of pressing research questions.

The undertaking was under the staff direction of Dr. Samuel A. Stouffer, who worked under the restrictions of a short time limit in order that prompt publication might be assured. He was assisted by Mr. Philip M. Hauser and Mr. A. J. Jaffe. The Committee wishes to express appreciation to the authors, who contributed their time and effort without remuneration, and to the many other individuals who generously lent aid and materials.

William F. Ogburn, Chairman
Shelby M. Harrison
Malcolm M. Willey

CONTENTS

Chapter I

Introduction

AS IS the case with so many of our social and economic problems, the national significance of internal migration became increasingly apparent during the depression. The purpose of this monograph is to survey briefly the ideas and facts as to depression migration, and to indicate the gaps in our knowledge. In order to accomplish this, a more general orientation in the subject is necessary. Therefore, this monograph, though focused on the depression, seeks to sketch more generally the nature of the problems of internal migration in the United States, to describe very briefly the data that are available for their study, and to indicate some of the more important types of additional materials needed if we are to make headway in better understanding and in solution of these problems.

It was perhaps inevitable, once the federal government began to assist in relief, that there would be a demand to move people out of areas where economic opportunity is meager and to assist them to locate in regions and communities where they would have a better chance to make a decent living. It was likewise all but inevitable that in the haste to get something done much would be done which would have little or no value in rehabilitating either the individual or the community. In general, Dr. Goodrich's critique of governmental policy (*Migration and Economic Opportunity*) is well founded. Much of what was done was ineffective at best and at worst was positively harmful. But it does not follow that because these hasty attempts at directed migration were mistaken, the proper policy is to let things take their course—laissez faire—or to encourage a continuance of just the same type of migration that we have had in the past.

There is a very general belief today that the United States has adequate resources to provide a good living, not only for our present population, but for any population we are likely to have for a long time to come. There is also a wide realization that some millions of people are now living in areas which are over populated in the sense that they lack the basic resources to supply a good living to their inhabitants. It follows, as a matter of course, that a redistribution of population—the need for which was accentuated by the depression because normal movements were somewhat retarded—is being advocated as one of the means to be used in assuring larger economic opportunities to the people living in these depressed areas. It is probably the interest in this aspect of internal migration which has made it a matter of somewhat general concern at the present time; for, certainly, we are not going to be in a position to direct migration to the greatest advantage of all, until we know a great deal more than we now do about its effects both upon the migrants and the communities involved.

The author does not pretend to have covered the field adequately; nor does he feel certain how much some of the studies he has suggested would contribute to the framing of a wise migration policy. There is always danger that the researcher will over value facts as such, or that he will forget the purpose for which the facts are being gathered. It is not improbable that the author has yielded to this temptation, in spite of his efforts to keep the problems of migration, as related to national welfare, in the forefront of his thinking in suggesting types of information needed.

At no point is any effort made to outline definite research projects. There are two chief reasons for this: (a) the incompetence of the author to do so in most fields, and (b) the belief that much less information that is useful can be secured by means of outlines which are not prepared with a definite situation in mind, than from those which are developed with the express purpose of getting information on concrete points.

Some readers may feel that the problems relating to mobility in the depression per se have been too much subordinated to the problems of mobility in general. The author urges, however, two considerations: (a) the problems of depression migration are different only in degree from those of migration at any other time; hence, they cannot be understood except in relation to the problems of migration in more normal periods; and (b) the data which can now be secured on many of the problems of internal migration in this country are very scanty.

In regard to the scope of the study, it was the author's understanding from the start that he was to focus on internal migration in the United States. Therefore, consideration of foreign immigration and of the experience of foreign countries in dealing with internal migration is excluded. The subject of foreign immigration and emigration is discussed in another monograph in this series, *Research Memorandum on Minority Peoples in the Depression* by Donald Young. Chapter III of that monograph contains also a discussion of internal migration with particular reference to minority peoples. Migration with reference to rural problems is treated also in *Research Memorandum on Rural Life in the Depression* by Dwight Sanderson.

Chapter II

Some General Considerations
on Migration

A S A background against which depression effects must be
studied, this chapter attempts to view internal migration in
a long time perspective.

Throughout human history all but a few individuals have
lived and died as members of some definite group. There have
always been some nonsocial individuals who lived more or less
as hermits, but the vast majority of men have spent their lives
as active members of a few more or less intimate groups, generally the same groups into which they were born. When individuals moved their abodes from place to place it was generally
because the clan, the tribe, or some other well organized group
to which they belonged was changing its place of residence. Even
among nomadic peoples the individual rarely left the tribe or
clan to strike out on his own among a different people. This
point need not be labored here because it is a generally accepted
fact.

The Social Significance of Migration

The consequence of maintaining such a close and continuing
relationship between the individual and his group was that the
individual had a familiar and stable social environment at all
times. Moreover, every group had in the course of ages developed a set of traditions—folkways and institutions—which
was more or less well adapted to its milieu, and the concurrence
in which by the individual insured a certain stability and integrity

4

of personality as well as of group structure. Individuals who broke away from their group were not numerous and they were generally looked at askance, not only by the group they had quitted but also by any other group to which they attempted to attach themselves. The person who did not have a definite position in the group and who, therefore, did not contribute to its welfare in the customary manner has always been an object of suspicion.

With the development of the division of labor and the improvement of transportation and communication the wandering of individuals from the family and tribal fold vastly increased. Hence, the amount of personal demoralization arising from the lack of strong personal ties to local groups has also increased, and the capacity of community institutions to direct the conduct of members of the community is often overtaxed. This prevents the firm establishment of customary modes of conduct and thus results in the development of unstable and uncertain personalities—people who neither know exactly what is expected of them nor how to achieve what is expected if they can find this out. Today there are many millions of people who have gone out from their family and neighborhood groups, generally in search of larger economic opportunity, who have thrown off the restraints not only of these small intimate groups, but also of the larger and more specialized groups, such as clubs, lodges, business associations, and labor unions.

Many of these persons have never been able to find a satisfactory place for themselves in the new community with its larger and less intimate groups. It is because modern migration is so largely individual, separating individuals from many of the established group contacts which give direction to conduct and meaning to activity, that it is of such great significance in modern life. The individuals and, even to a certain extent, the families which make up a modern community may be likened to the timbers which are destined to the framing of a ship. When each is shaped and put in place it performs a function and becomes an integral part of a useful whole, but when separated from the others or scattered in a storm it not only ceases to function as part of a useful vessel but becomes a menace to other vessels. In somewhat the same manner the person and the family, unattached to some community, wrenched out of integral organic relation to their neighbors and friends, become more or less anarchic and not only fail to perform social functions as adequately as they otherwise might, but they also interfere with the unification and effective action of the community as a whole. From the point of view of effective community organization, therefore, migration is of the utmost importance, since it seems to have been increasing rather steadily for a number of decades. It is true that the currents of migration have shifted frequently and that the measurable volume fluctuates considerably from time to time, but the uprooting of people from their families and neighborhoods and of families from other neighborhoods and communities goes on at a rapid pace. At one time, it may appear most prominently among the foreign-born, again among the southern plantation Negroes, while at yet another time it is most noticeable among the rural youth seeking a living and a fortune in the city, or even among those who are seeking a congenial climate in another part of the country. The nub of the *social* problem of migration, as distinguished from the economic problem, is the disintegration of personality and the inadequacy of the social organization of the community to guide conduct when migration becomes too great.

The problem of developing socially desirable types of personality through a well integrated social organization and of maintaining such a social organization becomes more difficult as the mental attitudes of the migrant individuals and the communities into which they move become more divergent. We speak of the problem thus arising as one of assimilation and it is generally recognized that this is more difficult the more the culture patterns of migrants differ from those of the receiving community. Thus, we have long recognized that foreign immigration created a more unmanageable situation than the migration of rural youth to neighboring cities. Recently it has also become apparent that southern Negroes settling in northern cities create problems quite different from and, in some respects, more difficult of solution, than those arising from the immigration of either the foreign-born or the native white rural youth. There is no need to elaborate these differences in the problems of adjustment or assimilation of these different migrant groups, for it is obvious that differences in language, differences in family customs, differences in standards of living, differences in attitudes towards government, differences in education, and many other cultural differences make integrated community life very difficult.

Some Economic Considerations

In general, it appears that the chief reason for migration of all kinds, international, interregional, intersectional and even, to a certain extent, local migration, is the desire to better the economic situation of the migrating group or individual. After making such a statement one should hasten to add that many individuals and groups have moved from their native homes to new locations because of other reasons, reasons which are as various as the interests of man in achieving a more satisfactory mode of living. But when all these multitudinous motives are taken into account, it yet appears that the economic motive has been and continues to be the predominant motive lying at the base of man's migratory movements. It can perhaps be said safely that migration is a process of social osmosis. It is one of the means which man has always used to establish a more satisfactory relation between his wants and his fulfillment of them. It is an attempt to equalize as best he can what he feels to be the unequal pressure of environment on individuals and groups.

Since we are concerned here only with internal migration within the United States, it may be well to point out, in general terms, some of the inequalities of pressure which lead men to move from place to place. A study of internal migration of population shows that for more than two and a half centuries, from the beginning of white settlement, the predominant migration was westward. Families were too large for all members to find farms in the home community, hence some of the children moved on to new land—to the West. At the same time there was a secondary movement from farms to towns and cities. Neither the westward movement nor the cityward movement was steady. There have been times when they were much accelerated as, for example, the westward movement in the era of railroad building following the Civil War, and the cityward movement in the period since 1890, and particularly since 1910. A careful study will show that the flow, whatever its direction and however great its magnitude, was towards what were believed to be greater economic opportunities. That this is just as true today, as at an earlier period, admits of no doubt. Indeed, there is much reason to expect that the greater the penetration of information regarding economic opportunities into the byways of the nation and the greater the ease of moving about within the nation, the more responsive people will become to regional economic differentials. Consequently it seems not improbable that the mobility of our population will increase, rather than decrease, for some time to come, even though the general economic development of the country becomes much more stabilized than it now is.

At present our most pronounced trends in migration are towards the great commercial and industrial centers, and the regions of exodus are very naturally the poorer and more backward agricultural areas. The great migratory movement is, therefore, no longer an east-west movement but a south-north and even a west-east movement. However, there is still a considerable migration to the far west from many parts of the country. The continued economic development of the nation along the lines it has followed in recent decades would lead one to expect that the migration from agricultural areas, and particularly from the poorer agricultural areas, to the commercial and industrial regions will continue for some time. The chief reasons for expecting this are as follows:

In the first place, the demand for agricultural products, for food and clothing, is much less elastic than that for most manufactured products. Hence, no considerable increase in agricultural population is to be expected in the near future because of increased demand for agricultural products unless there should be a marked increase in the general standard of living or in the size of our population. Since the growth of our population during the next few decades is practically certain to be very small as compared with the past, the demand for more agricultural products for direct human consumption must come chiefly from improvement in standards of living. It does not appear that this is likely to proceed at a pace that will call for any considerable increase in farm population under present conditions of farming, for:

In the second place, the mechanization of agriculture still proceeds, releasing products formerly fed to horses and mules to fatten cattle and hogs. Because of this mechanization, it is also reasonable to assume that as long as the farmer works his present long hours a smaller and smaller number of farm workers can supply the agricultural produce of the nation, unless new industrial uses for these products should develop rather rapidly.

In the third place, attention should be called to the fact that the agricultural population still has a goodly natural increase. It would increase by about 57 per cent in a generation, while most of the cities now have an intrinsic deficiency in births and within two or three decades will have more deaths than births unless birth rates rise rapidly. The cities will, therefore, demand more and more of the rural youth for their work. It is for these reasons that it seems reasonable to expect a continued movement of farm youth to the cities in the effort to equalize economic opportunity.

Finally, although the list is by no means exhausted, it is common knowledge that there are vast numbers of people in the mountain regions and in the poorer agricultural areas who are living at very low standards—indeed, at about subsistence standards. (There are over twenty-four millions living in the six rural problem areas as outlined by the Works Progress Administration.) It seems reasonable to assume, as Dr. Goodrich does, that several millions of these people can never hope for more than subsistence as long as they stay in their present homes and that these areas will probably be centers of emigration for many years to come.

In view of these considerations, there is every reason to expect that the social problems of migration will remain of great importance to the students of social science in the future as well as the present. Moreover, the practical and ethical problems will continue, necessitating decision as to whether the national welfare will be best served by allowing migrants to follow the long-time trend in migration into centers of industrial and commercial enterprise. A consideration of these practical and ethical problems must rest upon an inquiry into the economic and social factors underlying the redistribution of population—chiefly its urbanization, which has taken place since the onset of the industrial revolution. As such it would aim at finding out why our industrial and commercial enterprise has taken its present pattern of distribution and hence, why the pattern of population distribution is as it is. It would also go deeper and try to answer the question whether or not this present pattern is the best possible pattern, both from the standpoint of efficient operation of economic enterprise and from the broader standpoint of general social welfare. Manifestly such a matter cannot be treated merely as an aspect of internal migration but must be treated with all the broader implications continually in mind.

Significant Types of Migration

Movements from one place to another which do not much disturb the individual's social relations to his fellows, change his economic status, disturb the functioning of the institutions of the community, affect personal and community welfare, or upset the economic life either of the sending or receiving community, must be considered of little societal consequence.

In general, movements from one house or farm to another within the same neighborhood are of little social or economic significance either to the individual or the community. Even longer movements within or about a city or a farm community, which are in the nature of interchanges between communities of similar type, often involve no appreciable disturbance in the social and economic life of the individuals and communities involved. On the other hand, a move from one type of neighborhood to a different type only a short distance away may be decisive in moulding the lives of the persons involved and may also affect the development of the community.

In general, it is probably true that the greater the distance of migration the greater is the likelihood that there will be a complete severance of relations between an individual or family and the social milieu; and the greater the likelihood that serious problems of both personal and community adjustment will arise. Again, there can be no reasonable doubt that the person moving from a fairly simple uncomplicated environment into a more complex one, or vice versa, is more likely to encounter difficulties of personal adjustment than one who moves between communities which are fairly similar in structure and complexity. Furthermore, any type of migration may be significant from the standpoint of the community merely by reason of the numbers involved. Under existing conditions a large net migration from farms and villages means that the larger towns and cities are growing most rapidly. Consequently, an increasing proportion of the population finds itself in complex environments in which

social and economic adjustments are more numerous and difficult than those to which it has been accustomed. Rural-urban
migration has for a long while created many of our most difficult problems of personal and of community adjustment. It has
also thrown out of balance many of the social and economic
activities of the community. It has been, on the whole, a highly
disturbing factor in modern life, but it is quite impossible to
allocate the source of the disturbance accurately to the volume
of migration, to the change in type of social environment encountered, to the breaking of personal ties by the migrants, to
the general instability of the economic position of the migrants
or to any other single factor.

To place great emphasis upon the significance of rural-urban
migration is not to deny the importance of movement from city
to country or from city to city. It is merely to recognize that
such a large net movement in this direction, as has characterized
modern migration, cannot take place without introducing a
crisis into the lives of a considerable portion of the individuals
involved in this migratory movement and countless problems for
adjustment into the many communities.

Indeed, one would be making a serious mistake to assume
that the movement of families from cities to the abandoned
farms of some of our poorer counties does not create very serious
situations for these rural communities as well as for the migrants. In some rural communities, particularly those on the out-
skirts of cities, the provision of adequate schools for the children
of migrants is financially impossible. In others back-to-the-land
migration, even on a modest scale, swamps the governmental
and economic facilities, e.g., the established relief agencies. It
then becomes a serious matter and may lead to the development
of a submerged rural population.

It may be noted, however, that the back-to-the-land migrant is
probably coming back to a smaller community with whose people and organization he is more or less familiar. He finds his

adjustments, therefore, relatively easy as compared with the city-ward migrant who is more often going out into a strange, un-known, and more complex world. The city to city, or village to village migrant often, perhaps generally, goes among strangers, but he is keeping within a social structure of whose workings he knows something. The chances are that such a migrant will find problems of personal adjustment relatively easy unless they are complicated by the inability of the community to find an eco-nomic niche for him.

Where there is an abrupt change of occupation involved as well as a change of residence and a change in type of community (as is very frequently the case, especially in migration from coun-try to city) the difficulties of personal adjustment are inevitably enhanced and the economic problems of the receiving com-munity, due to the overcrowding of certain occupations, are often very great. In such occupational changes the fund of experience growing out of the past occupation frequently is of little value as a stabilizer of conduct in the new environment. Then, too, the economic instability of the migrant, resulting from this shift, often gives a certain direction to personal development which renders him ineffective in his new conditions of life. Thus the individual probably is more often left adrift in stranger waters when he changes abode, type of community, and occupa-tion at the same time, than he would be if he had changed but one at a time.

Enough has been said above to indicate that it is not yet feasible to set up criteria by which the significance of different types of migration can be judged. It seems that there is no type of migration which may not be of significance to the migrant and to the community under certain conditions. On the other hand, types of migration which at first might appear to be of great significance may be of negligible importance to many individuals and even to communities because of their own peculiar cir-cumstances.

General Character of Internal Migration in the
United States[1]

The population of the United States has always been a mobile population. From the time of earliest settlement there was a continuous and relatively large westward movement to new lands. Apparently, there was also a considerable movement from country to city in these early days. Although there are only scattered data before 1790, there is no reason to assume that this cityward movement began suddenly at that time. Since 1790 there is unmistakable evidence that the cities have grown much faster than the country as a whole. No doubt a part of this more rapid city growth came from the large proportion of immigrants stopping there, but an appreciable part of it must always have come from the surrounding rural areas. Aside from the general knowledge of the migration accompanying the settlement of the country it was not until 1850 that definite evidence of interstate migration became available. For that year tabulations of the state of birth of the native population became available and they have been secured at all subsequent censuses. These data, however, do not show the total movement of people from state to state during a given period but only the net results of this movement at a given moment.

In 1850, 24.0 per cent of the native-born were living in states other than those of their birth. This proportion rose to 24.7 per cent in 1860 and then declined steadily until 1900 when it amounted to only 20.6 per cent. By 1930 it had risen to 23.4 per cent, probably indicating an increased internal migration in recent years. We cannot be sure of this, however, because, as already noted, it is only the net result of all interstate migration that is recorded in the census. Some slight notion of the distance

---

[1] For a more detailed but concise statement of recent general trends in internal migration the reader is referred to Chapter III, "Trends in Population Redistribution," *The Problems of a Changing Population*. Washington: National Resources Committee. 1937

covered by all interstate migrants is found in the fact that only slightly less than one-half of all the people not living in the state of birth in 1930 were living in adjacent states, leaving somewhat more than one-half who had gone farther afield.

Until rather recently the chief currents of internal migration were from east to west. This is indicated by the fact that 10.1 per cent of the people born east of the Mississippi River were living west of it in 1890, while only 2.9 per cent of those born west of it were living east of it; in 1930, by contrast, these percentages were 6.6 and 5.4, respectively. During the decade 1920-30 the number of persons born west of the Mississippi River and living east of it increased by slightly more than 600,000, while the number of persons born east of the Mississippi River and living west of it decreased by about 80,000. However, the numbers involved in the east-west movement are three times as great as those involved in the west-east movement and people moving westward are probably older. Far more replacements would be needed to maintain numbers in the east-west movement than in the west-east movement. One can only say that *probably* the west-east movement is now greater than the east-west.

In the period since 1890, while the west-east has been creeping up on the east-west movement, the south-north movement also has been developing. In 1890, 5.8 per cent of the persons born in the South were living in the North. This percentage remained almost unchanged until 1910 when it was 5.3. Since then the number of such persons has more than doubled, and in 1930 the percentage was 8.6. This was the highest percentage for any of the large inter-sectional movements. The north-south movement, on the other hand, has grown but slowly. In 1890, 2.0 per cent of the people born in the North lived in the South and by 1930 this had increased only to 3.2 per cent. These figures on south-north and north-south movements are more significant if we remember that the former (south-north) is primarily from southern states east of the Mississippi River to northern states

east of it, while the latter (north-south) movement is chiefly
from northern states west of the Mississippi River to southern
states also west of it. The southern states east of the Mississippi
River have become increasingly a region of emigration towards
the North, while those west of the river have always been primarily a region of immigration, both from the southern states
east of the Mississippi and from northern states west of it.

Both whites and Negroes figure heavily in this south-north
movement. In 1930, 1,931,799 white persons and 1,355,789
Negroes born south of the Mason and Dixon line were living
north of it. This represents an increase since 1900 of 103 per
cent for whites and 304 per cent for Negroes. It is fairly safe
to predict that this south-north movement will continue to increase in importance, since it is in the South that the birth rate
remains high, while industrial and commercial development is
more rapid in the North. Even if there should be a more rapid
decentralization of industry in the future than in the past there
is no reason to think that *dispersion* (to use Goodrich's ter-
minology) will take place sufficiently rapidly to enable the sur-
plus population in the South to find jobs near home. But a
careful investigation of the trends in industrial development,
and particularly of the indirect community costs as well as of
the direct economic costs of various types of business enterprise
in different types of communities should throw considerable
light on the probable extent of future south-north and rural-
urban migration. Goodrich and Thompson[2] have already done
some excellent work in studying trends, but more needs to be
done. Furthermore, the writer does not think that Goodrich's[3]

---

[2] United States Bureau of the Census. *Location of Manufactures, 1899 to
1929: A Study of Tendencies toward Centralization and toward Dispersion of
Manufactures in the United States.* Washington: Government Printing Office.
1933. Prepared by Tracy E. Thompson.

[3] Goodrich, Carter, and others. *Migration and Economic Opportunity: The
Report of the Study of Population Redistribution, Philadelphia:* University of
Pennsylvania Press. 1936. Pp. 387 ff.

rather cavalier dismissal of the need of studying the freight rate structure as a factor in industrial location closes the question. It is the opinion of the writer that, although present trends in industrial development and in migration of population may continue, they are not necessarily permanent. We need to know whether, and to what extent, they rest on sound economic bases, if we are to judge probable future trends in migration.

As an example of what the state of birth data will yield for a particular state and city a brief analysis will be made of the data for New York state and city. Of the native urban population of 7,400,000 born in continental United States and living in New York state in 1930, 6,634,000 were born in the Middle Atlantic states and 6,240,000 were born in New York state. Of the 1,200,000 (approximately) native urban-dwellers who were not born in New York state, 233,000 came from New England, 393,000 from the other Middle Atlantic states, 143,000 from the East North Central states and 256,000 from the South Atlantic states. It would seem rather probable that much of the migration to urban communities in New York state from New England, the other Middle Atlantic states, and the East North Central states was from urban communities in those states. On the other hand, a large part of the migration from the South Atlantic states to urban New York state must have been from rural communities. It needs no argument to convince anyone that, by and large, the problems of adjustment and assimilation of rural migrants from the South to urban New York state are far more complex than those of migrants from either southern or northern urban communities. Furthermore, nearly one half of the migrants from the South to New York state were Negroes and nearly all of these went to urban communities. Obviously the assimilation of these southern Negroes into the life of the urban communities of the state is a far different problem from that involved in the assimilation of a like number of persons from the urban communities of New England.

Of the total white population of New York City 64.2 per cent was born in the United States, and of this about 87 per cent was born in New York state. Of the Negro population of the city, on the other hand, about 78 per cent was born in the United States, but of the native Negro population only 31 per cent was born in New York State. As would be expected, much the larger part of the native white population not born in the state came from nearby states, although there were considerable numbers from all parts of the nation. The Negroes not born in the state, of course, came from the South—especially from the South Atlantic states.

The examination of these state of birth data in detail will give a fairly adequate notion of the origin of the native population of a community at a particular time, but it does not provide any significant material on the demographic composition of the migrants, the length of their residence, nor does it give any hint as to the volume of migration year by year.

Chapter III

Depression Migration

FOLLOWING the cursory sketch in Chapter II of our chief migratory movements, attention will be turned to depression migration.

The Bureau of Agricultural Economics has estimated the annual movement of population to and from farms since 1920. Table I shows that since the War, at least, there has been a tremendous back and forth migration of population between country and city. The total movement to and from farms in the decade 1920-1930 amounted to more than thirty-four millions. Of course, many individuals are counted more than once in such

TABLE I
MOVEMENT OF PERSONS TO AND FROM FARMS:
UNITED STATES, 1920-1935[a]

| YEAR | PERSONS ARRIVING AT FARMS FROM CITIES, TOWNS, AND VILLAGES | PERSONS LEAVING FARMS FOR CITIES, TOWNS, AND VILLAGES | NET MOVEMENT FROM | |
			CITIES, TOWNS, AND VILLAGES TO FARMS	FARMS TO CITIES, TOWNS, AND VILLAGES
1920	560,000	896,000	—	336,000
1921	759,000	1,323,000	—	564,000
1922	1,115,000	2,252,000	—	1,137,000
1923	1,355,000	2,162,000	—	807,000
1924	1,581,000	2,068,000	—	487,000
1925	1,336,000	2,038,000	—	702,000
1926	1,427,000	2,334,000	—	907,000
1927	1,705,000	2,162,000	—	457,000
1928	1,698,000	2,120,000	—	422,000
1929	1,604,000	2,081,000	—	477,000
1930	1,611,000	1,823,000	—	212,000
1931	1,546,000	1,566,000	—	20,000
1932	1,777,000	1,511,000	266,000	—
1933	944,000	1,225,000	—	281,000
1934	700,000	1,051,000	—	351,000
1935	825,000	1,211,000	—	386,000
1920-1924	5,370,000	8,701,000	—	3,331,000
1925-1929	7,770,000	10,735,000	—	2,965,000
1930-1934	6,578,000	7,176,000	—	598,000

[a] United States Department of Agriculture, Bureau of Agricultural Economics, Farm Population Estimates, January 1, 1936. Released October 27, 1936. (Births and Deaths Not Taken into Account.)

movements but, even so, the number of separate individuals involved in rural-urban migration between 1920 and 1930 must have greatly exceeded the number of foreign-born entering and leaving the country during the same period. Unfortunately there is no way of knowing whether such a vast migration was peculiar to the 1920's or has been more or less normal for some decades. It seems not improbable, however, that this rural-urban migration has always been more important than was generally supposed.

Since 1930 rural-urban back and forth movements have declined, rather than increased as has commonly been assumed, if the data of the Bureau of Agricultural Economics are to be trusted. The total movement in 1930-34 was only 13,754,000 as compared with 18,505,000 in the preceding five years (1925-29). Thus this total migration between city and country was about 25 per cent less in five depression years than in the five preceding years. Even though the total migration, irrespective of direction, was less during the depression, the net movement either way might be proportionately quite different from that of previous periods. Consequently, there is no way to tell with any certainty just how rural-urban migration during the depression compares with that of predepression times. There is some reason, however, to believe that much of the talk of the back-to-the-land movement during the depression was without adequate foundation.

In this connection it would be of interest to make a special study of several typical counties in selected areas to find out just what the in and out movement was during the depression. Such a study would have to be made soon, if it were to be made at all, for memories grow dim and population changes are rapid. It may possibly be too late to make satisfactory studies even now, but the writer is disposed to believe that house to house canvass, together with the records of the county Agricultural Administration Act committees and the Soil Conservation committees, might yield some interesting and valuable results. Professor Lively's studies, which are referred to later,[1] are very suggestive and might provide a pattern for similar studies dealing chiefly with migration during the depression. But in order to get the most out of these studies, it would be necessary to make studies of the interchange of population between country and city under normal conditions. Without such comparative material we could not tell much about the effects of the depression on this interchange.

The Agricultural Census of 1935

The most extensive material now available on urban-rural migration during the depression is found in the Agricultural Census of 1935. It will be well, therefore, to devote some space to a critique of the data there presented.

The total number of persons living on farms in 1935 who lived in non-farm communities in 1930 was about 2,000,000, or slightly over 6 per cent of the farm population. This represented the number left on farms (as enumerated in the 1935 agricultural census) of the approximately 6,578,000 persons estimated by the Bureau of Agricultural Economics to have moved from non-farm to farm areas during 1930-1934. Unfortunately, no previous census has secured data on the number of people then on farms who lived in non-farm communities at an earlier time; hence no direct comparison can be made between 1935 conditions and those in earlier periods. Probably the number of persons moving to farms from non-farm areas has always been large, since so many city people were reared on the farm and were prepared to take up farming again if they cared to return to it. It would seem quite normal, therefore, to find a considerable number of people on farms at any given moment who were not on farms five years before. However, to find over 6 per cent of the farm population returning from non-farm territory in

---

[1] See page 30

five years is rather surprising; and, on the assumption that such a number of people moving from non-farm to farm areas was very unusual, this finding has been cited frequently as proof of the large back-to-the-land movement during the depression. There are two very serious difficulties with this interpretation. One is that we do not know whether or not such a back-to-the-farm movement is abnormal; and the other is that there is good reason to doubt whether 2,000,000 people actually moved to farm territory between 1930 and 1935.

The distribution of the population moving from non-farm territory to farms during the five years 1930-34 will throw some light on the probable nature of this movement. In the first place, the rural areas of industrial counties attracted a disproportion-ate share of the 2,000,000 referred to above and also of the total increase in farm population during 1930-34. Thus, although these industrial counties, located for the most part in the mid-eastern section of the country, contained only 21.4 per cent of the total farm population of the nation they accounted for 37.5 per cent of the migrants from non-farm to farm territory and for 64.3 per cent of the total gain in the nation's farm popula-tion. The most reasonable explanation of this large return move-ment to farms in the industrial counties seems, to the writer, to be that many people who were living on small acreage tracts in 1929 and were then working in urban communities were counted among the non-farm-rural population by the census enumerators in 1930; while the same persons (or others living in the same houses) who were without regular employment in 1934 were classified as farm population in 1935. Thus a large part of the gain in farm population in these industrial counties is not a bona fide increase in farmers. It represents, rather, a change in the classification of families between the 1930 population census and the 1935 agricultural census.

The author's bases for believing that the 1930 and the 1935 censuses are not altogether comparable are as follows:

(a) The Agricultural Census enumerators in 1935 had far more incentive to prolong their work than the 1930 enumerators, both because of some piece work pay in 1930 and because early in 1935 it was more generally felt that another job would be difficult to secure. This undoubtedly led to a more careful enumeration of borderline families as farm families in 1935 than in 1930. In 1930 every family was visited and enumerated for the population census, and even though the total pay would have been increased by filling out more farm schedules, the difference in remuneration may not have appeared worth the extra effort. (A good many men who are familiar with rural communities can cite rather convincing evidence that the census of 1930 was very deficient in their communities.) Besides, a man whose income came from factory work in a neighboring city in 1929 was probably not thought of as a farmer even though he lived on a place of more than three acres that produced more than $250 worth of food. In 1935, on the other hand, only an agricultural census was taken (covering operations during 1934) so that little pay was forthcoming for visits which did not consume enough time to fill in a farm schedule. Moreover, by 1934, many people living on small acreages had no source of income except their farming, or government work, or relief. There can be little doubt that many places which could have been properly counted as farms in both 1930 and 1935 were not so classified in 1930 but were placed in this category in 1935.

(b) The author has been at some pains to ascertain the opinions of 22 Ohio county agricultural agents regarding the large increases in their counties in number of farms and in population living on farms in 1935 which lived in non-farm territory in 1930. Practically all of these men believe there has been little or no increase in the number of bona fide farms in the county in which they are working. This is true without exception in the industrial counties and in the counties which lie close enough to industrial areas to draw people from them to settle on small

acreage tracts. Most of these men believe that the farm population increase in their counties arises from the classification of
places as farms in 1935 which were not so classed in 1930 or
from the more careful enumeration in 1935. In several cases the
agent says that he knows of no genuine new farm layout being
built in his county during this period. Of course such impressions do not constitute scientific evidence, but when they are
impressions of trained men who are thoroughly familiar with
farming in their county and who know a considerable portion
of the farmers personally, they are worthy of careful consideration. If a state-wide canvass of county agricultural agents could
be made in several states, and if these agents knew that their
state leader was interested in the enterprise, the results would
at least be helpful in judging whether it would be worth while
to carry the investigation further. Besides from such a canvass
it is possible that one would get some useful suggestions regarding methods by which the census results could be still further
tested. It should be mentioned also that the records of the county
Agricultural Administration Act and Soil Conservation committees might be helpful in this study.

(c) It is of interest, too, that in some of the Ohio counties
which had large increases in number of farms, there was a much
larger decrease in the average number of persons per farm between 1930 and 1935 than in other counties with small increases
in numbers of farms during this period. This would seem to indicate that a somewhat different class of persons was enumerated in the farm population in 1935 from that enumerated in
1930. A larger proportion of non-farm population which has
smaller families than the farm population would account for
this difference. The writer carried this particular investigation
only far enough to convince him that it would be worth while
to go farther. If the average number of persons per farm in all
counties, perhaps in all townships, were calculated, and then the
counties or townships were classified according to rate of in-

crease in farm population, degree of industrialization, proportion of farm workers, value of land, distance from city, and value
of farm products sold, it might throw considerable light on the
character of the increase in farm population.

Since there is no good reason to suppose that the situation in
the industrialized areas of Ohio is basically different from that
in other industrial areas in the northeastern section of the country, it appears highly probable that a considerable part of the
749,735 persons listed as living in non-farm territory in 1930
but as living on farms in these industrial counties in 1935, did
not actually move on to new tracts of land. The back-to-the-
land movement in industrial counties was almost certainly much
smaller than the crude figures indicate.

(d) The regions other than the industrial counties showing
a relatively large return migration are certain parts of the Southern Appalachian highlands, especially mining areas; portions of
the Ozarks; the cutover lands of Northern Michigan, Wisconsin,
and Minnesota; the far northwest; and scattered counties in the
Mountain states. There is reason to think that in these areas a
larger proportion of the population shown as moving from non-
farm territory (1930) to farms (1935) actually did move than
was the case in industrial counties. But there was certainly a
considerable number of men in these regions, who were earlier
engaged in mining and lumbering, who turned to subsistence
agriculture on small farms when their jobs in these other industries gave out. They were farmers only in the sense that they
had no other job at the time of the 1935 census. Hence, the one
and one-fourth millions returning to the land in the non-indus-
trial counties also included a goodly number who were not bona
fide farmers.

It is impossible to tell the exact effect on the total farm population of this increased inclusion of non-farm families among
the farm families in the 1935 census. It is not unlikely, however,
that a half or even more of the back-to-the-farm movement be-

tween 1930 and 1935 is spurious in the sense that it represents
a different classification from that employed in 1930. If this is
the case, the gain in total farm population during this period
must also be exaggerated by about the same amount. That is,
instead of a total gain of about 1,700,000 (comprising the reported gain of about 1,350,000, plus 300,000 or 400,000 to
allow for the fact that the enumeration in 1935 was in January
instead of in April as in 1930) the actual gain between 1930 and
1935 possibly did not exceed 700,000. Since the natural increase
of the 1930 farm population would have been about 2,000,000
by 1935, the net movement away from farms during the quin-
quennium was probably in the neighborhood of 1,300,000, or
about 250,000 per year, as compared with about 600,000 or
650,000 per year during the decade 1920-30. The important
point to remember is that there was still a fairly large net migration from farms during the depression, the common belief
to the contrary notwithstanding. The number of people who
moved to the farms during the depression was undoubtedly
considerably less than that leaving the farms for non-farm residences during the same period. So far as can be judged from
the available data, it is a great mistake to suppose that the migration back and forth between country and city was stopped by
the depression, or that this period, unlike the preceding decade,
was characterized by a large net back-to-the-farm migration.
There may have been a net backward movement in 1932 as
indicated by the Bureau of Agricultural Economics, but it was
much more than counterbalanced by the cityward migration of
other depression years.

If the 1935 agricultural census was more complete in its
enumeration of farm population than the regular 1930 census,
it is probable that most of the million persons here assumed to
have been enumerated in the 1935 census because of difference
in classification should have been enumerated in the same cate-
gory in 1930, so that the net gain in bona fide farm population

between 1930 and 1935 would be about the 700,000 estimated above. The vital point is that the relatively large gain in farm population shown by the 1935 census represents in part, perhaps to the extent of one-half, a census error, and not a genuine increase in the farm population which is to be attributed to a back-to-the-farm movement between 1930 and 1935.

From the above discussion it is clear that we must decide who is and who is not a farmer if we are ever to get comparable figures on the farm population from census to census. Without this we cannot expect to get a very accurate measure of actual migration into and out of farm communities. The probable differences between the 1930 and the 1935 censuses in classifying families as farm and non-farm families show the difficulties that now arise over the uncertainty of who is a farmer. This is a difficult question. It has given the Bureau of the Census much trouble and is likely to give it even more trouble as workers in cities move into the surrounding country. The writer does not feel competent to decide how it should be settled, but he has the temerity to make a suggestion or two about it.

If some definite plan of assigning an address to each rural house were developed it would be much easier to know whether or not new houses were added from census to census and whether they were farm houses or merely rural residences. It is possible, too, that if a question were asked in the census regarding the chief place of work of the head of the family, it would assist materially in assigning families correctly to the farm and the non-farm population. At the present time if a person lives on a farm he is ipso facto a farmer. This does not follow as a matter of course. A question regarding chief place of work or even the usual occupation would enable a distinction to be drawn between farmers and other types of workers living in the country on areas defined as farms by the census. It might not be necessary to ask such a question of every open-country resident. A sample secured in certain areas might throw a great deal of light on the extent to which non-agricultural workers live on tracts of land which are now classified as farms because of size or because of value of crops raised.

Under present conditions the census definition of a farm in 1930 and 1935 based on either the size of the land holding (three acres or more) or the raising of $250.00 worth of agricultural products is not a proper measure of the farm or non-farm status of the family and should be reconsidered. As has been indicated, it was possible that the same family on the same land was enumerated as a non-farm family in 1930 and as a farm family in 1935. The determining factor in the divergent classification was not the size of the holding or the worth of agricultural products but the non-farm employment or un-employment of the head. The proportion of one's time spent at farm work, one's usual occupation, and/or the amount of agricultural produce one sold (not used) would seem to be better measures of farmer status.

Migration to "Problem Areas"

It has also been quite commonly assumed that the return movement was very large, indeed almost overwhelming, in the areas least fitted to provide a decent living for their populations. This was not the case; or at least, if it were true in 1932 and 1933 it did not remain true in 1935, even according to the data provided by the Agricultural Census. As noted above, 6.6 per cent of the farm population enumerated in the 1935 census had lived in non-farm territory in 1930. In the six areas considered problem areas by the Works Progress Administration the 1935 farm population contained about 7 per cent of persons who had not lived on farms in 1930. This is only slightly higher than in the total farm population. It certainly cannot be regarded as showing any unusual movement back into these poor areas. Furthermore, the difference between the rate of return in the country as a whole and the problem areas is also very small if the industrial counties are left out of account, 5.2 per cent in the country as a whole and 6.0 per cent in the problem areas. By 1935, in any event, the net back-to-the-land movement in the problem areas was but little greater than elsewhere. Furthermore, the movement out of the problem areas was not smaller in proportion to the 1930 population than in the country as a whole. They showed a net increase aside from migration to farms of 1.1 per cent in the farm population, whereas the country as a whole showed a net decrease of 2.1 per cent, a total difference between the problem areas and the country as a whole of 3.2 per cent, or perhaps about 4 per cent between the problem areas and the remainder of the country. This difference is probably more than accounted for by the difference between the natural increase in population in the problem areas and in the country as a whole, since it is the problem areas where the birth rate still remains high. They can send out as many migrants in proportion to the base population as the better farming areas where the birth rates are relatively low, and still show an increase of population from an excess of births over deaths.

Tennessee Valley Authority Studies

As a possible further indication that the back-to-the-land migration of the depression has been exaggerated, it is of interest to note the results of two studies made of the families affected by the reservoirs being built by the Tennessee Valley Authority. Here it was found that in the Norris reservoir area in 1934, only 240 persons out of 2,836 families (perhaps 12,000 persons) had come back to the area after having had city or industrial work experience. In the Wheeler reservoir area, only 33 persons among 729 families (perhaps 3,000 persons) had had industrial work experience in other areas since 1920. It would appear that the total accumulated return movement in these areas did not exceed 1 per cent or 2 per cent. How much of this small movement is really the result of the depres-

sion cannot be told, nor can it be said that this sample is typical
of the region. But it makes one wonder whether the return movement into the purely farming areas of the Southern Appalachians has been as large as has generally been supposed. Perhaps
a study of relief rolls and of Agricultural Administration Act
records in a few typical counties would show how large this
return movement was.

Farm Mobility in Ohio

The mobility of farm population during the depression, outlined above, has been studied in some detail for a few townships in several states. Only the data for Ohio are available at
present. The following *Summary of Significant Findings* from
the Ohio study is quoted directly from a forthcoming bulletin
of the Ohio Experiment Station by Professor C. E. Lively and
Frances Foott.

The data of this bulletin were drawn from a field survey of 2,554
rural households located in ten rural townships and in eight villages.
Most of the area had been surveyed previously for similar purposes.
The mobility of the resident population and of adult children away
from the parental home was obtained, emphasis being placed upon
their movements during the period January 1, 1928 to January 1,
1935.

The analysis shows that, in the areas surveyed, there was a net loss
of population due to migration during the period 1930-35, except
in the northeastern, urbanized section. The general trend was similar
to that prevailing from 1920-30, except that the rate of net loss from
migration was only about two-thirds as heavy as it was during the
previous decade. This was partly a result of a slower rate of emigration and partly a result of immigration. The figures show that persons
reared in these areas shifted toward rural districts after 1929; that they
gave preference to villages as compared with the open country.

Households with the greatest mobility were those normal family
households composed of husband and wife, with or without children,
in which the head of the household was under middle age.

Relief families had 40 per cent more moves and 100 per cent more
changes of occupation than non-relief families.

There is evidence of an age cycle of mobility.

Apparently the economic depression failed to change the nature of the pattern of migration with respect to the distribution of migrants to country, village and city, although it did greatly reduce the volume of such migration.

Adult children migrating from the parental home before 1929 were living at home in 1935 at the rate of 33 per 1000 for males and 15 per 1000 for females. They left cities at the rate of 93 per 1000 who had migrated there. Females, children of village households and of relief households, emigrated at rates higher than average.

Of every 1000 children who were 10 years of age or over in 1929 and living at home, 654 were still living at home in 1935. Of the latter, 48 per cent of the males and 59 per cent of the females were 21 years of age or over.

In accounting for the accumulation of rural youth in the rural districts since 1930, failure to migrate may be regarded as a factor of at least twice the importance of return migration.

Male heads of families were continuously employed in 82.6 per cent of the cases. Of the others, 13.7 per cent were employed part of the time and 3.7 per cent were not employed at any time. The median number of months of unemployment was 29.2.

The process of occupational change consisted largely of an attempt on the part of wage workers to avoid unemployment and to obtain an occupational status of greater economic security. In order to accomplish this some shifted toward agriculture. Many who were unable to do this swelled the ranks of the unemployed. The gross occupational pattern of adult children who left home before 1929 was not markedly disturbed. However, children of migratory age after 1929 were seriously retarded in their occupational advancement.

Between 1928 and 1935, every farm operator that left farming was replaced by three persons who were not farm operators in 1928. These new operators were drawn chiefly from the skilled, semi-skilled and unskilled occupational classes.

In a general way these detailed studies bear out the broad conclusions already stated. There was no large back-to-the-farm movement in these Ohio townships during the depression. Indeed there was a net loss in farm population except in the highly urbanized area (the industrial counties) in the northeastern part of the state. There was not even any considerable backward movement of adult children who had left home before 1929, only 33 out of each 1,000 males and 15 out of each 1,000 females. Clearly there is nothing startling in these findings. The mobility of population in Ohio during the depression was of much the same general character as it had been in preceding years although it was probably considerably less in amount.

These findings suggest the possibility that in a period of depression those who are so fortunate as to escape unemployment hold on to their jobs much more tenaciously than in normal times, so that the total mobility of residence and occupation is less in depression periods than at other times.

This problem certainly needs careful investigation. It seems not unlikely that the records of educational institutions might show how turnover in staff in depression times compared with that in pre-depression periods. Also the records of the employment departments of business concerns should show the rates of turnover during these two periods and possibly the types of people involved. Of course such records probably would not show much about migration but they might show the attitudes of people toward holding their jobs at these times, which would indirectly indicate their mobility.

Perhaps the most important source for data on factors immobilizing population during the depression are to be found in the relief practices of different communities. Before the federal government entered the relief field it is generally believed that aid was largely confined to local residents and that transients were relieved only to the usual extent. The whole question of the effect of the relief policies of local, state, and federal governments upon mobility needs thorough investigation. There is a very common belief in some quarters that differences in relief policies had a great deal to do with migration into and out of certain areas. Even though it is rather doubtful whether conclusive evidence of population changes growing out of relief policies can be produced, it certainly is important that this matter be studied most thoroughly. It is possible that the distribution of population in the country may be rather markedly affected by the relief policies adopted. It would be highly desirable to know what we are doing in this respect.

The Village in the Depression

Professor Lively's information regarding the movements of farm population and of the children of these people during the depression suggests, as already noted, that some of what has been called the back-to-the-farm movement was really a back-to-the-village movement. At first glance Brunner and Lorge's re-study of 140 villages[2] seems to confirm this conclusion. Almost without exception their investigators reported that the villages had gained new families between 1930 and 1936. For all the villages the estimated gain in population was 6.67 per cent. During this same period the population of the United States increased about 4.3 per cent, hence, these villages grew about one-half faster than the country as a whole and about twice (or more) as fast as the farm population, if the above analysis is correct. But villages have a larger natural increase than cities and should increase apart from migration, faster than the country as a whole. Hence, the writer is disposed to think that the 6.67 per cent in the villages is not far from what their increase would have been in 1930-36 (not 1935) if there had been no net migration into or out of them during this time. This is not to dispute the movement of families into these villages during the depression, but merely to point out that the population of these villages probably was little if any larger in 1936 than was to be expected from their natural increase alone. It turns out then that the above-mentioned study of villages does not provide as conclusive evidence of net migration to villages during the depression as at first appears. Nor does their finding of a still more rapid increase in the population around the villages

[2] Brunner, Edmund de S. and Lorge, Irving. *Rural Trends in Depression Years.* New York: Columbia University Press. 1937. The author had the privilege of reading Chapter III on population in advance of publication.

prove a rapid back-to-the-land movement, since the area is not the same in 1936 as in 1930. It is quite impossible, therefore, to say what part of the gain in this area might come from natural increase, what part from added area, and what part from migration.

Professors Brunner and Lorge made use of school enrollment in getting the estimates of population in these villages and, although they also had actual counts taken in 45 of them, their judgment was that the estimates in which school enrollment played an important part, perhaps a decisive part, were the more accurate.

In view of the fact that school censuses and enrollments are coming into more frequent use for estimating populations in intercensal years, there has been included in Chapter IV of this monograph a discussion of their value for this purpose.

State Censuses

A cursory examination of the South Dakota state census of 1935 suggests that in that state, at least, there was less migration to farms than to villages during the period 1930-35. In some counties the villages gained in population during the period 1930-35 while the county as a whole lost population. This suggests the need for finding out from where the families moving into the villages came. The Brunner and Lorge study shows that most of them came from the surrounding open country rather than from nearby urban centers. This would appear to contradict the very general belief that there was a large back-to-the-village movement from the cities. It may be that a careful study of the South Dakota and Florida censuses of 1935 will throw some light on this problem, although additional tabulations would have to be made from the original schedules.

Furthermore, whether these state censuses are comparable with the federal census only a careful study will reveal. Besides, even if there were greater migration toward villages than toward the open country in South Dakota and Florida, it is not at all certain that the same movement existed in other states.[3] South Dakota has been especially hard hit by drought in recent years and the organization of relief might be responsible for any difference in village and farm growth which might be revealed by such a study. Furthermore, the steady increase in the mechanization of farms may have more effect in reducing farm population in this state than in most other states. Finally, Florida is always a special case because of the peculiar composition of migrants to a resort area. But the 1935 state census of South Dakota and also that of Florida should be studied carefully to see whether they throw any light on migration into or out of these states and their several types of communities during this depression period.

Urban Mobility

Another type of mobility about which some information is available is the movement of city populations. A few facts will suffice to indicate the general character of this type of migration.

Rather extensive data are available for Cleveland, Ohio. In 1933 about thirty families out of each 100 living within the Cleveland Metropolitan District moved from the place in which they were living at the end of 1932. Most of these (90 per cent) moved about within the Cleveland Metropolitan District. About 4 per cent moved from the Cleveland Metropolitan District to other parts of the United States, and about 6 per cent to the Cleveland Metropolitan District from other parts of the United States. Of the families moving within the Cleveland Metropolitan District 31 per cent stayed in the same census tract.

In 1934 the total movement and the proportion of the total population moving was not so large, while the proportion moving into and out of the city from other areas was larger. The most significant difference between 1933 and 1934, however,

[3] Other states which have taken censuses since 1930 are: Kansas, Rhode Island, Michigan, Massachusetts.

was the increase in the proportion of the families "undoubling."[4] Apparently, larger incomes increased the number of moves arising from the desire of the families to live by themselves. It appears that in Cleveland from one-fourth to one-third of all families move each year and that about two-thirds of those who move about within the city cross a census tract boundary. Even though, on the average, every family in the Cleveland Metropolitan District moves once in three or four years, there are many families that have lived in their present residence for many years. Thus the Special 1935 Report "Standards of Living in the Cleveland Metropolitan District" shows 18,462 or 6 per cent of the families in the Cleveland Metropolitan District to have lived in the same quarters for 20 years or more; 48,285 or 17 per cent for 10-19 years; 57,881 or 20 per cent for 5-9 years; and 167,563 or 57 per cent for less than five years.[5] The stability of the Cleveland population is somewhat greater than indicated here, because the six per cent of the families who have lived in their present residence for twenty years or more constituted far more than six per cent twenty years ago. In the very nature of the case a community growing rapidly by migration from outside will have a very high proportion of families that have lived less than twenty years in the same house. But even so no one can doubt that the problems of developing community solidarity or civic spirit are aggravated when 57 per cent of all families have lived in their present abodes for less than five years.

[4] Care must be exercised in working with data on "doubling up." See Stouffer, S. A. and Lazarsfeld, Paul F. *Research Memorandum on the Family in the Depression.* Chapter IV reports "practically a zero correlation between doubling up, by tracts, as given in the local Real Property Inventories (Green, Howard Whipple. *Real Property Inventory of the Cleveland Metropolitan District,* Cleveland, 1936, Report No. 9) of 1933 and 1934 and doubling up as reported for Cleveland in the *Federal Real Property Inventory* as of January, 1934." These results are attributed to differences in definition of "extra families."

[5] Green, Howard Whipple. *Movements of Families within the Cleveland Metropolitan District, 1934.* Cleveland: Real Property Inventory of Metropolitan Cleveland, Report No. 5, P. 19. 1935

This same study shows that home ownership is a potent factor in increasing the stability of the population. Comparison of the length of time owner families have lived in their present abodes with that of all families as given above shows that "16,685 or 14 per cent of them had lived in the same quarters for 20 years or more; 40,578 or 34 per cent for 10-19 years; 40,090 or 33 per cent for 5-9 years; 23,735 or 19 per cent for less than 5 years."[6]

An interesting aspect of this study of city mobility is the movement from one economic area to another. In general it may be said that this moving about from place to place within the metropolitan district is accompanied by a rather surprising amount of change to districts having a different average monthly rental. When the census tracts of the Cleveland Metropolitan District are arranged in fourteen monthly rental groups, the percentage of families moving into each group during 1933 in terms of the number of families living in this area in October, 1932, is shown below.

$10–$14	10.2	$45–$49 . . . . . 17.4
15– 19	11.6	50– 54 . . . . . 20.0
20– 24	8.6	55– 59 . . . . . 19.6
25– 29	11.1	60– 64 . . . . . 20.0
30– 34	14.1	65– 74 . . . . . 18.7
35– 39	11.9	75– 99 . . . . . 12.4
40– 44	12.7	100 and over 10.0

The movement was largest proportionally into areas having rentals from $45 to $74 but was largest absolutely in the areas with rentals of $25 to $49, the mode being found in the $35-$39 group.

It is also of interest to note that the proportion of families that moved into areas with higher average rentals than in their area of previous residence was, as would be expected, very high

---

[6] *Ibid.*, page 19. Federal Real Property Inventory schedules contain data from which similar analysis can be made for the sixty-four cities covered in that survey.

among those moving into areas having rentals of $15 to $29. The proportion that moved from these areas into lower average rental areas was correspondingly low. Those who moved to areas with rentals of $30-$39 from cheaper areas just about balanced those who moved in from better areas. Among all higher rentals the movement into relatively cheaper areas from more expensive areas was larger than the movement from cheaper into more expensive areas. Tables II and III show the percentages moving from more expensive areas into cheaper areas and vice versa for all of the fourteen monthly rental groups.

It is impossible to say just what social significance attaches to the mobility of population within a metropolitan district, which has just been described. It seems reasonably certain that moving from districts where the average rent is under $30 a month to districts where it is over $50 and, vice versa, indicates, in many instances, a considerable and rather sudden change in economic status, which would be likely to affect family life very materially. However, this change of residence from an area with one average rental to another does not necessarily indicate a corresponding change in the family rental. Furthermore, only 580 families made this much of a change in moving to higher rent areas and only 589 made a similar step downward in choosing new districts. Thus only 1,169, or 3.2 per cent, of the 36,816 families moved outside the same rental group to which they belonged in October, 1932, that is, moved into rental groups averaging $20 higher or lower than the one which they left. It is clear that much the larger part of all migration outside the original rental group was to another group having a monthly rental only a few dollars different. Without knowing vastly more than we do now about the characteristics of these moving families it is hard to believe that such a change in the average rental of the area into which one moves will of itself have any significant effects upon the life of the family.

TABLE II

PERCENTAGE DISTRIBUTION OF FAMILIES MOVING FROM EACH ECONOMIC AREA, BY AREA TO WHICH THEY MOVED CLEVELAND METROPOLITAN DISTRICT 1933[a]

Area Moved From:	Area Moved To:														Percentage Families Moving to:		Percentage Families in Oct. 1932 That Moved Out of Areas in 1933
	Lowest	2	3	4	5	6	7	8	9	10	11	12	13	Highest	Better Areas	Worse Areas	
Lowest	—	26.38	37.42	14.72	9.82	5.52	4.91	1.23							100.00	—	20.48
2	2.55	—	33.52	20.58	6.56	21.22	6.19	4.37	2.82	1.00	.27	.64	.27	—	97.44	2.55	14.96
3	1.22	11.22	—	34.81	11.70	23.78	10.63	2.19	1.00	1.41	.96	.78	.26	.04	87.56	12.44	11.39
4	.16	3.74	18.23	—	23.11	25.82	13.31	6.16	1.35	3.08	2.29	1.12	1.52	.09	77.85	22.13	12.58
5	.19	1.62	6.35	28.14	—	31.99	15.74	6.35	1.49	4.73	1.75	1.10	.45	.10	63.70	36.30	15.31
6	.08	2.42	6.45	14.53	13.25	—	33.63	10.33	4.22	5.83	3.78	3.47	1.38	.62	63.26	36.73	11.78
7	.02	1.18	2.07	7.16	6.05	30.34	—	21.04	9.05	9.82	5.75	3.64	3.04	.85	53.19	46.82	12.43
8	—	1.00	1.39	4.76	3.39	13.48	35.88	—	12.39	8.76	8.88	5.61	3.88	.58	40.10	59.90	16.28
9	.06	1.14	.60	2.64	1.80	7.38	20.11	17.95	—	18.67	13.63	8.22	6.78	1.02	48.32	51.68	16.57
10	—	.42	.88	4.13	3.19	10.09	15.14	10.93	9.95	—	20.74	14.37	7.92	2.24	45.27	54.73	18.82
11	—	.32	.64	2.35	1.15	8.28	11.22	11.36	9.20	22.91	—	19.92	10.53	2.12	32.57	67.43	17.34
12	—	.39	.28	1.57	1.06	7.71	8.11	8.05	5.03	22.53	22.86	—	15.32	7.10	22.42	77.59	16.09
13	—	.15	1.05	2.84	.75	7.26	11.82	6.43	5.09	13.31	14.51	21.17	—	15.63	15.63	84.38	11.05
Highest	—	.39	.39	1.57	1.38	8.66	9.06	2.76	3.15	9.06	8.86	19.09	35.63	—	—	100.00	8.77

[a] Green H .W., *Movements of Families Within the Cleveland Metropolitan District 1933*

TABLE III

PERCENTAGE DISTRIBUTION OF FAMILIES MOVING TO EACH ECONOMIC AREA, BY AREA FROM WHICH THEY MOVED: CLEVELAND METROPOLITAN DISTRICT, 1933[a]

Area Moved From:	Area Moved To:														Percentage Families Moving From:		[b]
	Lowest	2	3	4	5	6	7	8	9	10	11	12	13	Highest	Better Areas	Worse Areas	
Lowest	—	5.05	3.00	.63	.56	.15	.13	.06					.20		99.99	—	10.18
2	34.57	—	18.13	5.96	2.54	3.84	1.14	1.36	1.54	.37	.12	.34	.47		94.94	5.05	11.61
3	40.74	35.56	—	24.78	11.14	10.58	4.80	1.67	1.34	1.28	1.04	1.01	4.33	.17	78.87	21.13	8.56
4	8.64	18.78	38.47	—	34.90	18.22	9.53	7.49	2.88	4.43	3.91	2.31	.69	.69	68.62	31.37	11.15
5	7.41	5.87	9.66	22.90	—	16.28	8.13	5.56	2.29	4.90	2.16	1.64	.52	.52	50.87	49.14	14.07
6	6.17	17.02	19.06	22.98	28.02	—	33.74	17.60	12.57	11.76	9.06	10.02	5.53	6.41	50.94	49.07	11.92
7	1.23	8.10	5.96	11.04	12.48	29.28	—	34.97	26.34	19.31	13.45	10.26	11.86	8.67	42.53	57.47	12.70
8		3.87	2.27	4.14	3.95	7.33	19.80	—	20.33	9.71	11.70	8.91	8.53	3.29	31.29	68.71	17.38
9	1.23	2.23	.49	1.16	1.06	2.03	5.60	8.49	—	10.45	9.06	6.60	7.53	2.95	32.71	67.29	20.01
10		1.41	1.23	3.11	3.21	4.74	7.22	8.86	14.12	—	23.63	19.75	15.06	11.09	37.80	62.21	19.63
11		.82	.69	1.34	.88	2.97	4.08	7.01	9.94	16.73	—	20.86	15.26	7.97	25.87	74.13	19.98
12		.82	.25	.74	.67	2.27	2.42	4.09	4.47	13.54	16.33	—	18.25	22.01	18.30	81.70	18.67
13		.23	.69	1.00	.35	1.60	2.64	2.44	3.38	5.98	7.74	13.63	—	36.22	12.06	87.95	12.40
Highest		.23	.10	.21	.25	.72	.77	.40	.80	1.55	1.80	4.67	12.06	—	—	99.99	9.97

a See note[a], table II
b Families moving into area in 1933 as percentage of families in that area in October, 1932

It seems probable, therefore, that, on the whole, factors other than change in the average rent paid in the areas into which the family moves will be found exercising the major portions of any disturbing influence which intra-city migration may introduce into the lives of the city's dwellers. At present we can only guess at what these other factors are: changes in occupation, development of a new circle of friends, increased intimacy with business associates, the joining of a labor union, and the many other changes in group life which are a common feature of modern city living.

In the writer's judgment only intensive case studies may reveal the significance of intra-city migration. What are the effects on individual attitudes of mind of moving about within a city? How is the school attainment of the children affected? Does a marked change in economic and social status affect intra-city migration and, if so, in what ways? Do areas which show a high degree of mobility have special problems and, if so, what are they? Is there need of special institutional development in areas of high mobility? It is not unlikely that a study of the records of the public utilities (water, gas, electricity, telephones) would show the areas of high mobility within a city, but they would have to be correlated with many other factors, e.g., the residence of persons arrested, the residence of relief cases, the residence of those registered in the employment exchanges and many other factors before we could be sure of any close connection of migration with certain urgent social and economic problems. Even should such a general connection be shown, it will be necessary to make the intensive case studies referred to above before we can be sure what the problems of migration are.

The data for Cleveland are interesting to the student of mobility primarily because of their bearing on intra-city moves. Another source of migration into cities is the unemployment census of Cincinnati taken in the early summer of 1935. Nearly

one-third of the population of Cincinnati was born outside of
Ohio and of these non-Ohioans about one-third were born in
Kentucky. Indiana furnished the second largest contingent with
Georgia, Tennessee, Alabama, and Illinois following in the
order named. When white and Negro migrants are considered
separately there are marked differences in origin as would be
expected. Kentucky is well in the lead in supplying both whites
and Negroes. Indiana is second in supplying whites but Georgia
is second in supplying Negroes. The other states supplying large
numbers of Negroes are Alabama and Tennessee.

It is also of considerable interest that except for the year preceding May 31, 1935, the number of white migrants into the city
during the depression was as large or larger than in predepression years. Among Negroes there seems to have been a more or
less steady decline year by year for almost ten years.

The proportion of out-of-state migrants was much higher
among Negroes than among whites. Whereas about one-fourth
of the whites came from outside the state about two-thirds of
the Negroes were migrants. Of the whites only a little over one-
half had been in the city ten years or more, while about two-
thirds of the Negroes had been there ten years or more. In all
categories female outnumber male migrants but their preponder-
ance is more marked among whites than among Negroes. Unfortunately, age data are not available, hence, the age at time of
migration to Cincinnati cannot be told.

It is possible that other cities which took censuses during the
depression have somewhat similar data with which these could
be compared to find out whether migration into Cincinnati followed the same pattern as in other cities.[7]

_____

[7] Other cities which have taken censuses since 1930 are: Aberdeen, Wash-
ington; Bellingham, Washington; Bridgeport, Connecticut; Chicago, Illinois;
Cincinnati, Ohio; Dayton, Ohio; Everett, Washington; Seattle, Washington;
Spokane, Washington; Tacoma, Washington; Toledo, Ohio; Utica, New York;
Yakima, Washington; as well as cities in states cited earlier in this chapter,
which took a state census.

Chapter IV

Problems and Methods of Research

IN THE preceding chapter the types of data available on population movements during the depression were indicated and their limitations were discussed. In this connection a number of problems which arise in the study of migration were considered. In this chapter these and additional problems and methods with which the student of migration must deal are examined, primarily from the standpoint of new research which is needed.

The Michigan Unemployment Census

Perhaps the most significant mobility data yet collected during the depression are those in the sample study of the Michigan unemployment census.[1] Through the courtesy of the Works Progress Administration (Division of Social Research) and of the Emergency Welfare Relief Commission of the State of Michigan the author has had access to the schedule forms and to some of the preliminary tabulations of this study.

A number of important problems on internal mobility during the depression will be illuminated by these Michigan data. Among these are: What were the differences in the frequency and range of migration (intra-county, inter-county, inter-state) of workers classified by marital status, age, urban-rural place of

---

[1] The first bulletin dealing with mobility is: "Geographical and Occupational Mobility of Gainful Workers," *Michigan Census of Population and Unemployment,* First series, Number 8, State of Michigan, Lansing, April 1937. This bulletin, however, reports limited data on the mobility of unemployed workers only.

residence, urban-rural direction of movement, type of community (city size, open country, village), class of occupation, employment status, and by cross classifications of these characteristics? What were the differences in movements among heads of multi-person families, other workers in such families, and unattached workers?

It will be possible to analyze these Michigan data on movements by time of occurrence—year by year from April 1, 1930, to January 1, 1935. Such an analysis should be made to trace mobility through the period studied. It would be well also through such analysis to check the reliability of the reporting of movements. Faulty memory of the persons interviewed or inadequate inquiry on the part of enumerators may result in an increase of relatively short moves as the time of the census (January 1935) is approached.

Unfortunately, we have no direct means of finding out in what respects, if any, the mobility of this Michigan population between April 1930, and December 1934, is different from mobility of similar groups in predepression times. Nor can we even say whether the percentage moving at all is different from the normal migration in these groups. It is possible, however, that, when the complete data for the Michigan unemployment census are available, comparisons between the composition of the population in the same areas in 1930 and 1934 will show what the depression did both to induce migration and to change the composition of the population in different types of communities. Since the writer does not know exactly what data are being tabulated nor the areas which were enumerated, he cannot, of course, tell what comparisons can be made nor how valuable they will be.

If the data from the Michigan census are in such form that the agricultural population of certain townships can be compared with the farm population enumerated in the 1935 agricultural census, it is possible that the virtues and deficiencies of the latter can be checked rather closely for these areas. For example, if a comparison of the data from these two enumerations taken within a short time of one another were made in detail, it might show whether or not people who thought of themselves as unemployed non-farm workers in the Michigan unemployment census were classed as farm people by the agricultural census. Where the two censuses checked sufficiently well to inspire confidence in the results it would also be possible to get some idea of the changes, in the comparison of the population between 1930 and 1935. This in turn might throw some light on net migration during this interval and the type of people migrating. In particular it might show the effects of migration during this period on sex and age makeup of different types of rural areas, such as those near industrial cities and those in depressed mining areas and in some of the cutover regions. How far these comparisons can be carried depends entirely upon the data to be made available; but in any case the studies would have to be sampling studies, since the Michigan Unemployment Census was a sample census and the 1935 Agricultural Census deals only with a particular group. At the best, therefore, comparisons of depression and predepression migration in Michigan must leave much to be desired, although they should be much superior to those possible in most other areas.

Sample Censuses

It would appear that for the future there would be a very good chance to get some valuable data to compare with these Michigan data for depression years if the Bureau of the Census could be persuaded to take some sample counts in Michigan in connection with the regular decennial census of 1940. This raises the whole question of sample censuses which needs to be thoroughly considered before the 1940 Census. Because of its very great importance for future research in the whole field of population this matter should be discussed at some length.

The Bureau of the Census has always taken the position that it could not take sample censuses in particular areas—that what it did must be done for the entire country or not at all. This position is justifiable, no doubt, as long as the task of the Bureau is confined to providing for administrative bureaus information which is needed for all political subdivisions. If, however, the government finds that it continually needs new information on many aspects of population growth and distribution in order to advise Congress on matters of public policy, then it would appear that the Census Bureau must either prepare to become a research agency as well as a counting agency or some other bureau must be created to investigate, in whatever way seems most possible, all kinds of population movements which may affect national welfare.

Any student of population questions knows that the providing of information on population for policy-making purposes does not require that a complete canvass of the population be made on every point on which information is needed. Smaller but more intensive sample studies will often provide more useful information when carried out by skilled investigators, than will much more comprehensive data secured by less competent workers. It appears to the writer, therefore, that the time has come when the Bureau of the Census should seriously consider the carrying out of a number of sample studies, some at the time of the regular census and others at intervals between censuses.

It would be wise to begin now to provide adequate migration information for certain typical areas so that it would be available in the future when it is needed for comparative purposes; for, as has been indicated in several places, most of such information is extremely difficult to secure after the event, and some of it cannot possibly be secured after the lapse of several years.

As an example of the type of material that might be gathered in an intensive sample study, it may be pointed out how valuable it would be to know the chief points in the migration history of certain groups of people, in cities, in rural areas, and in villages in certain regions. The schedules for gathering such data would not be as complicated as those frequently used in cost of living studies and in field investigations carried out by the agricultural colleges. The information would, of course, have a great deal more value if tabulated in conjunction with regular census data.

Migration and Population Estimates

One of the most important contributions that can be made to the study of migration at the present time is the estimation of the mere volume of migration from and to the various areas and regions of the United States. From what has already been said, it will be realized that our knowledge of the volume of depression migration must come to a considerable extent from such estimates. It will not be out of place, therefore, to devote some space to the discussion of methods by which such estimates may be made and to pointing out their limitations.

The first step in working out estimates of migration is to secure totals of the population at a given time. Therefore, it will be necessary to make a short critique of the methods used for estimating intercensal populations.

The method of estimating intercensal populations for given areas within the country which has attracted, perhaps, most attention recently is the use of changes in the school census and school enrollment as a guide to changes in population from year to year. Brunner and Lorge used the data on school enrollment in estimating the 1936 population of the 140 villages studied. The Bureau of the Census has also made some use of these data in working out intercensal estimates for states and cities. Thornthwaite, likewise, used it in some of his work on the *Study of Population Redistribution*.

One difficulty in using the school census to estimate popula-

tion in many states is that the basis for the support of schools
has been changing quite rapidly. As a result, it often becomes
more important now than formerly to enumerate all children,
and, if state aid is given on the per capita basis, it may even be
to the advantage of the particular community to pad its school
census. This may apply to any size of community. Furthermore,
in many small communities the school census is so uneven from
year to year that it is highly unreliable as a measure of population changes. This criticism probably is not so applicable to
larger communities. Since using the school census as a basis for
estimating total population assumes that the children enumerated in it are a fixed proportion of the total population, it is of
least value when there is most migration, because it is just at
that time that their ratio to the rest of the population is likely
to be changing most rapidly. Table IV shows how the proportion of persons 5-19 years of age changed between 1920 and
1930 in certain cities.

In the cities of over half a million there were very wide varia-
tions in the accuracy with which the total population of 1930
could have been calculated from the proportion of persons 5-19
years of age in 1920. (The 5-19 age group does not correspond
exactly to the group included in the school census or enrolled in
the schools, but it seems highly probable that the correspondence
between these two groups of young persons is relatively close.)
Assuming that the school census, or enrollment, could be used
as well as the 5-19 group, and that it had not varied between
1920 and 1930, the populations of Chicago and Los Angeles
could have been calculated to within 1 per cent of the 1930
census figure by using the proportion of persons in the school
census of 1920 to the total population of that year to calculate
the 1930 population. In Detroit, however, this method would
have led to an overestimation of the population by more than
12 per cent and in San Francisco to an underestimation of 7.6
per cent. In the smaller cities the range of variation in accuracy

on prediction would have been about as great. Clearly this method yields very uncertain results even when applied to rather large populations. Since the proportion of migrants to total popu-

TABLE IV

PERSONS 5 TO 19 YEARS OF AGE AS PERCENTAGE OF TOTAL POPULATION IN 1900, 1910, 1920 AND 1930 AND PERCENTAGE CHANGE FROM 1920 TO 1930: SELECTED CITIES[a]

CITY	PERSONS 5 TO 19 AS PERCENTAGE OF TOTAL POPULATION				PERCENTAGE CHANGE 1920 to 1930
	1930	1920	1910	1900	
Baltimore, Md.	26.0	25.6	27.3	29.4	1.6
Boston, Mass.	25.2	24.6	25.0	23.8	2.4
Buffalo, New York	26.8	25.7	—	—	4.3
Chicago, Illinois	25.2	25.4	26.8	29.0	−.8
Cleveland, Ohio	27.8	25.8	26.7	30.0	7.8
Detroit, Michigan	25.7	22.9	—	—	12.2
Los Angeles, Calif.	20.1	19.9	21.0	—	1.0
Milwaukee, Wis.	25.4	25.9	—	—	−1.9
New York, N. Y.	25.2	26.4	27.7	27.9	−4.5
Philadelphia, Pa.	26.0	27.8	26.3	26.7	−6.5
Pittsburgh, Pa.	27.8	26.9	27.3	29.2	3.3
St. Louis, Mo.	22.9	24.1	25.9	29.2	−5.0
San Francisco, Calif.	18.3	19.8	—	—	−7.6
Newark, New Jersey	28.1	27.5	—	—	2.2
Rochester, New York	25.7	24.1	—	—	6.6
Toledo, Ohio	24.6	24.2	—	—	1.7
Atlanta, Ga.	27.0	26.3	—	—	2.7
Providence, R. I.	27.4	25.7	—	—	6.6
Worcester, Mass.	27.1	25.3	—	—	7.1
Hartford, Conn.	25.9	24.3	—	—	6.6
Springfield, Mass.	25.6	23.4	—	—	9.4
Long Beach, Calif.	20.5	19.6	—	—	4.6
Norfolk, Va.	26.7	24.6	—	—	8.5
Chattanooga, Tenn.	28.2	25.7	—	—	9.7
Fort Wayne, Ind.	24.5	24.7	—	—	−.8
Wichita, Kans.	25.2	24.9	—	—	1.2
Peoria, Illinois	22.7	22.8	—	—	−.4
El Paso, Texas	29.3	29.6	—	—	−1.0
Duluth, Minn.	27.7	26.2	—	—	5.7
Pueblo, Colo.	25.9	26.9	—	—	−3.7
Oak Park, Illinois	21.8	24.0	—	—	−9.2
Covington, Ky.	24.5	25.1	—	—	−2.4
Dearborn, Mich.	27.5	19.3	—	—	—[b]
Lincoln, Nebr.	26.0	25.3	—	—	2.8
Mt. Vernon, N. Y.	24.8	26.8	—	—	−7.5
Cleveland Heights, Ohio	24.0	22.6	—	—	6.2
Lancaster, Pa.	25.0	24.6	—	—	1.6
Port Arthur, Texas	27.7	28.7	—	—	−3.5
Racine, Wis.	26.9	24.7	—	—	8.9
Tampa, Fla.	28.2	30.1	—	—	−6.3

[a] United States Bureau of the Census, decennial Census of Population.
[b] Boundary changes make data not comparable, see Fifteenth Census of the U. S., Vol. 1, Population, p. 532, footnote 36.

lation is relatively small, and since the growth in population less natural increase is all attributed to migration, the error in estimating migration into these cities would be several times as large as the error in estimating total population. The error in estimating migration into Detroit would have been from 30 to 50 per cent. A method which yields such variable results and which cannot be checked until after the next census must be used with extreme caution.

What has just been said about difficulties in using the school census to estimate population and migration applies also to school enrollment, with certain additional chances for error, particularly in small communities. School enrollment may be quite appreciably affected by the changing of bus routes, the closing of one or more neighboring schools, the topping off of a grade or two in the smaller schools and sending the children in the higher grades to another school, and various other factors which may not affect population at all.

All these difficulties should not deter one from experimenting with school census and enrollment data as a guide to population estimates from which migration into or out of a community could be deduced, but when the size of error is very large, as it apparently is in many communities, it is very doubtful how much use should be made of the results. It would appear that the character of the migration itself may have considerable effect on the proportion of children in the population (Los Angeles and Detroit) so that it would seem to be necessary to know something about the changes in the composition of migrants before one could be reasonably sure what changes in the proportion of children to population are taking place.

There is certainly need for further investigation into the usability of school census data in estimating intercensal populations, but because of local peculiarities this must be done for each community separately before much reliance can be placed on the results. It seems obvious that the larger the population of the unit to which it is applied the more likely is this method to yield useful results. For states and for the nation as a whole it may be very useful; it may prove to be of less value for cities and for smaller communities. Even when the school census is used as one of the elements in state estimates, some of the results suggest that it may not be very satisfactory in estimating differentials in migration. For example, it is very difficult to understand why Indiana should have an estimated increase in total population, 1930-36, larger than either Illinois or Ohio, both of which have much larger populations and larger absolute natural increases.

In a period of depression, it is especially difficult to use school census or enrollment figures for population estimates, because it is highly probable that they vary more than the total population and because the ways in which they vary from the normal are unknown. The Michigan Unemployment Census, as has already been noted, may give some clue to the ways in which the comparison of the population in various types of communities is affected by migration, but we can not tell yet. Smaller sample studies also will contribute information along this line but, as was pointed out in the case of Lively's and Brunner's studies, generalization from a few samples is highly hazardous. This is one reason·that census sampling on a larger scale is stressed as an important method for the future study of migration.

If migration is to be measured at any given time, other than by actual census count, population must be counted or estimated and the change in numbers since the last count or estimate must be apportioned between natural increase and migration. In many smaller places it has been impossible heretofore to get at natural increase because of the failure to allocate births and deaths to the usual place of residence. In the future reliable information on this point will be somewhat more abundant, so that it should be possible to indicate what part of the population of a community has migrated if the total population is known.

It has been suggested that the data on changes in the numbers of water, gas, and electric meters and telephones might show the population changes in a city and, also, that intra-city movements of families might be derived from records of meter changes for customers. It has already been suggested that these records might be useful in arriving at relative amounts of mobility in different sections of the city, but it appears somewhat more doubtful whether the number of meters and telephones in use is a very satisfactory measure of total population.

It seems rather obvious that, in a period of depression, the number of meters in use is likely to decrease much faster than the population because of the doubling up of families. As evidence that doubling up is important one may cite data from the Chicago Census of 1934. The number of families in Chicago in 1934 having subheads was about 65,000 or almost 8 per cent of all families. Since such information is not available for pre-depression periods, it is not known how this compares with such a period as 1929. Presumably it is much larger, and, since most of these families doubling up had meters removed, it is reasonable to assume that a count of meters would exaggerate the movement of people out of the city. This view is at least made to appear reasonable by data on intra-metropolitan district moves in Cleveland in 1933 and 1934. In 1933, out of a total of 79,069 families moving within the metropolitan district, 4,117 or 5.21 per cent were undoubling moves. In 1934, the figures were 65,334 and 6,069 or 9.29 per cent, respectively. It would appear that in a period of depression or recovery, changes in the number of meters would be a very dangerous guide to increase or decrease in a city's population, although it might be useful in a period of sustained prosperity.

Difficulty would also be encountered in keeping track of intra-city moves by use of the records of meter movements. As a result of doubling up in a period of depression, the companies' records of family movements would be far from complete. They would lose track of many families entirely so that their movements could not be traced. In a period of undoubling these same families would appear as new families, although it is possible that they could be traced back to the time when they had their last meter removed. In prolonged periods, during which similar economic conditions prevailed, it is probable that much information regarding intra-city movement could be secured from these records. In other words it would appear that the records of public utility companies would be particularly unreliable as a source of finding out about population and migration changes at the very times when we are likely to be most interested in these changes.

It is possible that city directories, when recently compiled, could be used to estimate population with fair accuracy. The following-through of certain selected names over a period of years might also yield some information regarding intra-city migration, but, since the directories are not always issued with sufficient frequency, this is rather doubtful. The use of the names in the directory as a basis for estimating population would generally, perhaps always, involve the use of an average number of persons to each address. This number might vary considerably from time to time, but, even so, it would seem to the writer that the results were more likely to be within a reasonable limit of error than when the number of meters in use is the basis for the estimate.

Methods of Estimating Migration

Since there has been very little information showing directly the amounts of migration into and out of different communities, it has been necessary to resort to estimates. Two methods have been used in making these estimates, both of which are based on census population or on estimated population. The first is that of calculating the net change in the population of an area during the intercensus period which would be expected from an excess of births over deaths if no migration occurred and then comparing natural increase with the observed increase in the population. The difference between the two presumably represents the net immigration into or the net emigration out of the community of persons during the interval. If age data are available in the censuses the migration by age can be estimated.

There are obviously a number of difficulties that arise in applying such a method. In the first place, it assumes that the registration of births and deaths is either fairly accurate or can be corrected to give reasonably accurate results for the communities studied. The errors arising from this assumption probably are not so great as to invalidate the results for practical purposes.

In the second place, it assumes that the errors in the census in reporting age either are not serious or can be allowed for, so that a calculated age group can be compared with the same census age group. Thus, it assumes that since the survivors in 1930 from the age group 40-44 in 1920 would be 50-54 they can be compared with the census group of this age to determine whether the community has gained or lost population of this age by migration. Unfortunately, people have rather marked preferences in reporting their ages, their nativity, and even their color to the censustaker. The result is that the census group of a given age, nativity, and color is not entirely made up of the survivors from the same nativity or color group ten years younger at the preceding census, even if there is no migration into or out of the group.

This method can be used in estimating migration in any area for which birth and death registration is adequate and population data are available—states, cities, counties, and even smaller communities. In this respect it has a distinct advantage over a second method, discussed below.

The second method has been used by a number of people to calculate the intercensus migration between states for the native population. It consists in dividing the number of native whites or Negroes of a given age in the entire United States at the beginning of a decade (1920), into the population of the same group ten years older at the end of the decade (1930), thus securing survival rates for each age group of the native population (white or Negro). These survival rates are then applied to the similar age groups in each of the states at the beginning of the decade, and the results are subtracted from the census population at the end of the decade to determine the amount of the in or out migration which has occurred in these groups in the state during the decade.

This method of calculating a survival rate for the native population of a given age assumes that the native population of the United States of this age is not affected appreciably by emigration or immigration; i.e., that the native white population 40-44 in 1930 is made up of the survivors of the native white population 30-34 in 1920. This is probably substantially true, although there is reason to think that at certain ages the native white population is appreciably increased by foreign-born persons who report themselves as natives; also, there is some movement into the native white population of persons who reported themselves as Negroes and Mexicans at the preceding census. It is further assumed that the survival rates in each state are the same as in the United States as a whole. This should not introduce much error in most states at the ages at which most migration takes place, but it is a source of error which should not be overlooked. Thus, in 1931, the survival rate of males 35-39 to 45-49 in New York state was 1.2 per cent below the rate for the United States while that for the same group in Kansas was 2.6 per cent above that for the United States. Clearly the use of the United States survival rate tends to underestimate the migration into New York state and to exaggerate that into Kansas.

In the application of this method, the errors in reporting age to the census also operate to exaggerate migration at certain ages and to understate it at other ages, but probably the errors here are not as serious as in the first method. Perhaps the most serious drawback in the use of this method is that the error is likely to be considerable when the United States survival rate for the native population is applied to cities and, indeed, to any relatively small group.

Changes in the Motivation of Migration During the Depression

It is generally taken for granted that people migrate (excluding movements within the same economic area) to improve their economic condition. Does this motive change any during a depression? Does desire for security take the place of desire for improvement, and, if so, how does it affect migration?

These questions might be answered by a variety of studies, but the writer is disposed to think that intensive case studies would throw more light on the changes in motivation of migration during a depression than most types of more extensive statistical study.

The Works Progress Administration study on migrant families furnishes some statistical data on this particular group, but as long as it stands alone there is no means of comparing depression and predepression motivation. Many people may feel that motivation is not a proper object of scientific study, but until we do know why people move and what kinds of attraction or expulsion are operative in migration, it is hard to see how we are going to formulate any migration policy which will work and still be democratic.

The writer would suggest not only studies on differentials in economic opportunity in relation to migration but also case studies and questionnaires calculated to show what kinds of people move to what kinds of communities and for what reasons, and how well different types of migrants succeed in these varying circumstances. After all, the migration of people will be determined by their judgment of what is to their advantage and this advantage may not always be calculated in economic terms. No policy can succeed which is not based on enhanced individual (and family) opportunity. It behooves us, then, to know whether economic opportunity is the only kind that need be taken into account, and whether motivation is so different under depression conditions that different policies can be carried out then from those which are feasible in more normal periods. If the desire for economic security, to a certain extent, replaces the desire for economic advancement during a depression, how will this affect migration? Perhaps an intensive study of some of the non-farm rural communities which have grown up during the depression will help us to understand better the factors which determine the direction of migration. The writer can see no other way of getting at any changes in motivation which may have taken place.

Assimilation

The ability of different communities to assimilate immigrants is a matter of the greatest importance, but, unfortunately, one about which we know little. Clearly we are not in position to develop practical migration policies until we do know something about the capacity of different types of communities to assimilate different types of people. It is possible that this capacity is different in periods of depression. If so, we should know in what respects it is different in order to adjust migration policies to altered capacity.

The ability of a community to support its institutions (schools, churches, lodges, clubs, and so forth) is certainly affected by a depression. Does this in turn affect its assimilation of migrants? It seems probable that a study of the institutions of two communities showing different capacities to assimilate migrants of the same general character, might throw much light on the relation between community institutions and assimilation. In order to get at depression differences, this study should be extended to cover the depression period. It is not improbable that some highly important principles of assimilation might emerge from the study of differences in assimilation in depression and non-depression periods. Such a study would involve comparison of the functioning of schools, churches, lodges, labor unions, and so forth; also of the organization of personnel relations in the industries and commercial enterprises. It would also be of the

greatest importance to study the leadership in all kinds of activities in these communities—leadership in economic enterprise, in
politics, in education, in cultural undertakings, in labor organizations and in any other fields where leadership seemed to be of
importance, since there is little doubt it affects functioning of
community institutions and their capacity to assimilate migrants.

Then, it would probably be well to study in the same way
communities with different types of migrants—Negroes, Scandinavian farm youth, mountain whites, and other important
groups—to find out how the presence of these different groups
affects the functioning of a community. The type of investigation needed to answer these questions is again the intensive case
study. Only after case studies are completed will it be possible
to outline statistical studies to the best advantage.

Migration and Natural Increase

The relation between migration and natural increase is one
of the most important in the whole field of population problems,
but up to the present it has received only the most casual attention.[2] Many population problems of the depression are involved.

The general pattern of the differential birth rate is well
known. As regards the size of community there is a marked inverse relation between size of the community and level of the
birth rate—the larger the community the lower the birth rate.
Within a community the pattern shows a decided inverse relation
between economic and social status and the level of the birth
rate—the better the economic and social position of the family
the lower the birth rate. As a group, the cities of 25,000 and over
in 1930 were failing by about twenty per cent to reproduce themselves, i.e., they were only raising about four-fifths enough
children to keep up their numbers when their age composition
became adjusted to their birth rates.

---

[2] For research on depression birth rates see Stouffer, S. A. and Lazarsfeld, Paul
F. *Research Memorandum on the Family in the Depression.* Chapter V

Bearing these facts in mind, and also bearing in mind that the prospect, judging from present trends, is for a still further concentration of population in and about the cities of over 25,000, the question arising is whether such facts should have any weight in searching for a migration policy.

It is not intended to enter into the arguments for and against the desirability of a further increase in population, nor to discuss the prospect of the disappearance of these differentials in the near future. The writer will be dogmatic to the extent of saying that he believes the rural-urban differentials in natural increase are likely to persist for some time; also that the distribution of our population as between urban communities and rural communities will continue to have an effect upon the growth of our population. If this is the case, then it is an important fact to bear in mind in working toward a migration policy, no matter whether one believes that we have already passed the optimum population in this country or whether one thinks that we need to maintain a fairly large increase for some time to come.

Of course, if one believes that the present differential birth rates will soon disappear, the rural-urban distribution of population becomes a matter of no significance from the standpoint of population growth. Unfortunately, we have only opinion to guide us on this matter at the present time, because we know so little about the reasons why rural people have larger families than urban people. All that is urged here is that we should not ignore the probable effects of migration policy upon the growth of population in the nation.

We should investigate the effects of migration into different types of communities upon the reproduction of the migrants. If movement into large cities has a different effect from movement into villages then it may become a matter of public interest to encourage one type of migration rather than another. It is in studying such a matter as this that some special sample censuses would be of value. If the future growth of population during the next few decades is closely bound up with the direction and the amount of migration, as seems not unlikely, then it becomes a matter of importance to control migration so that it will not nullify other public policies affecting the growth of population.

Migration and Education

Discussion in earlier pages of depression mobility should have made it clear that there is a significant relationship between educational problems and migration.[3] Within the nation, people generally move from regions of restricted to those of larger economic opportunity. But, as already pointed out, it is in the regions of narrow opportunity that the birth rate is highest and the proportion of children of school age to productive adults (20-60 years of age) is largest. Hence, our rural-urban migrants come preponderantly from areas in which educational opportunity is at a minimum. The result is that a very considerable portion of the migrants to the cities are inadequately prepared to take part in the more complex economic, political, and social life of the cities where they will spend the larger part of their adult lives.

The writer would suggest that studies be made of the educational equipment needed by migrants to cities if they are to become good citizens, and that these requirements be compared with what the children are actually getting in the high birth rate areas from which they are migrating. Here again it would appear that intensive case studies would probably give us the most useful information. On the face of it, it is absurd to expect that boys and girls, possessing what may be a reasonably adequate elementary education for subsistence hill-farming or even for general farming on the better lands of the Middle West, are

---

[3] For suggestions for research in education see monograph in this series by The Educational Policies Commission, *Research Memorandum on Education in the Depression.*

fitted to take their places in the modern city as economic units, as parents, and as citizens. Once it is determined what education migrants need and what they are getting, the question of how the gap between them can be bridged will come up for decision. This is not within the province of this discussion.

Migration and the Distribution of the National Income

The relation between migration and the distribution of the national income is of importance both because of the large movement of young adults to the city about the time they reach productive ages, and because of the large proportion of the estates of many farmers which passes into the hands of their children who have moved to the cities. A careful study of farmers' estates probated in a number of counties in different regions should show what portions remain in the country and what go elsewhere. It might also be possible to secure from these data on estates some estimates of the amount of the annual income of farmers which goes in interest payment on mortgages contracted because of migration of children from farms to cities. The writer does not feel that he is competent to do more than pass on these general suggestions on this point.

The moving of young adults to the city also removes some of the rural investment of the rural community to the city, for it certainly costs $1500 to $2500, even under the most modest conditions, to raise a child to the age when he can go to the city to look out for himself. Each migrant, therefore, may be looked upon as a donation of capital by the rural community to the city. It would be interesting to know what taxes the city would have to pay to be used by rural communities for education, health, and so forth in order to bear their proportional share of the cost of providing their migrant adult workers. Certainly it would run into amounts which would make present contributions to state educational funds and federal funds used in rural communities look pitiably small.

Migration and the Law

There is a legal aspect of internal migration in the depression which needs investigation, although it can scarcely be regarded as primarily a problem of the movement of people. In the study of internal migration in the United States there has been no need heretofore to discuss the legal rights of people to move from state to state. Presumably, United States citizenship carried with it the right to move about within the United States as one saw fit. However, it appears that some of the states have advertised their attractions too well and have found themselves burdened with migrants who had no independent means and who were almost certain to be unable to find jobs.

In what appears to the layman to be an illegal manner, California and Florida have denied indigent migrants the right to enter the state and have hastened the departure of dependent migrants who had secured entrance in spite of the attempts to turn them back at the border. Such state action constitutes a problem of grave importance from the standpoint of civil rights of United States citizens and needs very careful investigation. Does the fact of being a citizen of the United States imply the right to move freely from state to state, or is this only a right of those citizens who also have a certain economic status? It is of the utmost importance to know how far state's rights extend in the control of migration. It would seem that the investigation of this matter would fall within the province of the constitutional lawyer rather then of the social scientist. But it seems clear that planned migration is going to come squarely up against the question of whether a state can close its borders to any United States citizen and, if so, under what conditions.

Extensive Statistical Studies of Migration

In what follows a few of the more practicable suggestions for keeping track of the volume of migration will be discussed briefly. These suggestions do not specially relate to the study of depression migration. But since the same types of studies would be equally informative regarding both depression and non-depression migration they deserve consideration.

It has been suggested that at the next regular census (1940) the question should be asked: Where did you (and the members of your family) live at the time of the 1930 census?—(state, county, city, township, farm, or non-farm.) For tabulation pur-poses it has been proposed to divide the country into 300 or 400 areas and make cross tabulations between all these areas. Such data would show the net result of the migration of the past ten years from each of these areas to all the others, and when used in conjunction with the regular census information on age, sex, nativity, etc., should give a comprehensive picture of the chief currents of net migration and of the composition of these currents. These areas would be so plotted that the larger cities would be tabulated separately and it is also probable that two or three tiers of counties around the larger cities would be treated as separate areas.

The difficulties of such a tabulation would be very consider-able because of the large number of areas requiring cross tabula-tions. But even with 400 areas it would be impossible to secure as high a degree of homogeneity in population within each area as would be desirable.

Such a census of net migration between 1930 and 1940 would be of great value. It would enable us to see the net results of ten years of migration in great detail and would show the nature and magnitude of the problem as no lesser study could do. It would also show the composition of the migrating population in great detail and would, thus, set before us, in a clear light, many of the differences between migrating populations in dif-ferent communities which we can only surmise at the present time. The cross tabulations of the personal characteristics of migrants, of their movements, and of occupations from such a census would provide a great deal of information on some of the economic aspects of migration. It might also throw light on the changes in the occupations of migrants from one census to another, if the 1930 schedules of certain selected groups of migrants could be matched with their 1940 schedules.

But with all the information such a census of migration would supply it would tell us nothing about the frequency of movement, or the length of residence of the migrant in different communities. Besides, as is probably inevitable in any census taken as ours is, it would almost certainly omit entirely a considerable proportion of the most highly migratory part of our population—those who do not stay put long enough to get counted by a visiting enumerator.

Finally, valuable as such a migration census would be, it would contain almost no information on the problems of personal adjustment and community assimilation which are among the most important of all those connected with migration. One can but wonder whether it would not be much wiser to spend the same amount of money on sample censuses in certain carefully selected areas. These samples could be canvassed much more thoroughly for personal consequences of migration, for history of individual and family migration and for changes of occupation. Before any such sample study would be possible the whole policy of the Bureau of the Census would have to be altered as has already been explained.

For some years, as noted above, the Bureau of Agricultural Economics has gathered data on the movement of population to and from farms. For this purpose it has used a select list of crop reporters. The Bureau is well aware that its data are unsatisfactory in many respects and is anxious to improve them. Just how this can be done remains to be seen. Only those thoroughly familiar with what is now being done and with the contacts of the United States Department of Agriculture with the farm population are in position to suggest practicable improvements. But here, as in most other cases, there is not the least doubt that better data can be obtained if sufficient money is available. Another method by means of which a large amount of current information about migrants might be secured is through the change of address material collected by the Post Office Department. Whenever there is a change of post office address the migrating individual (presumably the head of the family), in order that he may receive mail at his new address, would be given a card by the postmaster in the community he is leaving which must be filled out and given to the carrier in his new home. The information called for on these cards presumably would show whether the person expected to stay any length of time at the new address, enough personal description for identification (e.g., age, sex, and occupation) and, of course, community of origin and destination. These cards could then be turned over to some central agency for tabulation (the Bureau of the Census) which would issue periodical bulletins giving such information on migration as was available. In order to put such a scheme into operation and make the record of migration significant, it would probably be necessary to use some divisions of the country similar to the three hundred or four hundred areas referred to above.

It would appear that such a scheme should be fairly simple to operate, would yield much more accurate results than that now in use by the Bureau of Agricultural Economics, and would have many advantages over the census scheme described above. It would enable the government to keep a current account of the volume and the direction of migration which would be very valuable from a number of standpoints.

Another possible source of information about migration is just now being opened up in the registration of persons under the Social Security Act. It is too soon to say whether the information gathered for insurance purposes will be of much value for the study of migration; but it is hard to see how people can be kept track of for purposes of insurance without their full migration history. Then, too, the other information needed for the pur-

poses of administering this act should be of much value in the
study of the social and economic characteristics of the migrant
population. In the near future this may prove to be one of the
most important sources of information about migrants, and its
importance should increase directly as social security is extended
to include more and more of the population.

The records of employment exchanges which must be dove-
tailed with those of the Social Security Board, if unemployment
insurance is to be made effective, should also yield valuable information on migration. Not only should these records show
the amount of migration within the past few months, but they
should also show the occupational history of those registered
over rather long periods of time. They should furnish much
valuable information to the researcher in migration.

When one contemplates the migration data needed by the
various governmental agencies and the variety of information
regarding individuals and families which they must assemble,
one is inclined to think, that in the not distant future it will be
more economical and more satisfactory to have some central
agency which will keep a complete record of every individual
from the cradle to the grave much as is now in effect in
Holland. Such a complete record of individuals and families
would supply much of the statistical information regarding migration that is needed for its study and control. No doubt there
will be some opposition to such a scheme of universal and continuous population accounting, but it appears that, in any event,
we must have most of this information for a variety of administrative purposes in our complex modern world. If this is the case,
it may not be many years until it will be made available, also, for
research purposes. But it should not be forgotten that abundance
of statistical information regarding migration is not to be desired
on its own account. It is only important to the social scientist, as
contrasted with the administrator, if it enables him to understand better the problems of personal and community adjust-

ment arising out of migration, and to suggest better means of controlling its volume and direction in the interests of human welfare. But statistical studies of migrants, no matter how complete, can never be entirely satisfactory. We must also have psychological and sociological studies of migration which will yield knowledge of mental attitudes and adjustments.

In speaking of psychological and sociological studies the writer refers, on the one hand, chiefly to studies of the changes in and the development of mental attitudes in migrants, and, on the other hand, to studies showing the growth, adaptation, and functioning of social institutions in the presence of migrants. The case studies referred to in several places above should yield much information of this character. Such studies are necessary both because they will aid in the interpretation of the quantitative materials which may be gathered, and because they will help materially in the more precise determination of the data on migration which ought to be gathered by special studies as well as by administrative agencies.

The ultimate purpose of studies in migration as in all other aspects of community life is to provide knowledge leading to better understanding and, therefore, to more intelligent control of human conduct. Expressed in these general terms, studies in migration may seem to have little significance. But it is highly probable that these studies will lead to some concrete results which will be of direct benefit to migrants and to the communities affected by migration. If from a study of the economic aspects of migration we could learn what communities can be expected to absorb new migrants and in what numbers they can absorb and assimilate them some progress will have been made. If, in addition, it can be learned what types of communities offer the best conditions for the personal development of migrants, still another step will have been taken in the formation of a sound migration policy. Further, if any significant relation between migration and population growth can be found these two aspects of population movement can be harmoniously linked together.

It may be, as Professor Goodrich seems to believe, that laissez faire is the best policy with regard to migration. It may be that the following of present trends is the most intelligent policy possible. Yet the writer does not believe that we are in position to say, in the present state of our knowledge. Because the depression efforts at directed migration to date have been of questionable value, it does not follow that we cannot do better when we have more information regarding the social and economic factors involved in migration. Nor can it be assumed that the present pattern of economic organization which, of course, determines in general the volume and direction of internal migration, is the best possible pattern even from the standpoint of efficient production and distribution—to say nothing of the possibility that personal and community life might be greatly enriched by a different distribution within the nation. It may be so, but there is sufficient evidence of accident, inertia, and arbitrary conduct in the building of the present pattern of population distribution to make it appear advisable to carry out some very intensive and extensive investigations into the factors creating this pattern before we conclude, from our depression experience, that laissez faire is the best policy with regard to internal migration.

Selected Bibliography*

ALBIG, WILLIAM. "A Comparison of Methods of Recording Urban Residential Mobility." *Sociol & Social Res* 22:226-33 Ja '37

————. "A Method of Recording Trends in Urban Residential Mobility." *Sociol & Social Res* 21:120-27 N-D '36

————. "The Mobility of Urban Population: A Study of Four Cities of 30,000 to 40,000 Population." *Social Forces* 11:351-67 Mr '33

ALLIN, BUSHROD W. and PARSONS, KENNETH H. "Changes in the School Census Since 1920." *Land Policy R* 1, Sup 1 Je '35. A publication of the Agricultural Adjustment Administration.

————. "Rural-Urban Migration in Relation to Land Quality." *Land Policy R* 1:9-12 Mr '35. A publication of the Agricultural Adjustment Administration.

ALLRED, C. E., LUEBKE, B. H., and TOSCH, C. A. *Mobility of Rural Relief Families.* Works Progress Administration cooperative plan of rural research, Report No. 14

"American Migration, Significant Changes in Place of Residence." New York Trust Company. *Index* 12:217-22 N '32

ANDERSON, W. A. *The Mobility of Rural Families, I.* Ithaca: Cornell Ag Exp Bul 607 Je '34

————. *The Mobility of Rural Families, II. Change in Residence and in Occupation of Sons and Daughters in Rural Families in Genessee County.* Ithaca: Cornell Ag Exp Bul 623 '35

————. *Movement of Population to and from New York State.* Ithaca: Cornell Ag Exp Bul 591 Ap '34

————. *Population Trends in New York State, 1900 to 1930.* Ithaca: Cornell Ag Exp Bul 547 D '32

ANDERSON, W. A. and LOOMIS, C. P. *Migration among Sons and Daughters of White Farmers in Wake County, North Carolina, 1929.* Raleigh: N C Ag Exp Bul 275 Je '30

* The author wishes to make special acknowledgment of the kindness of Dr. Dorothy Thomas in allowing him to use her bibliography on migration. He is indebted to her for about one-fourth of the titles listed here.

ASCH, BERTA. *Farm Families on Relief and Rehabilitation.* Washington: Works Progress Administration Research Monograph No. 6 '36

BAKER, O. E. *The Future Need for Farm Land.* Washington: Bur Ag Econ, U S Dept of Ag. Addresses at Farm and Home Week, Iowa State College, Ames, Iowa F 9 '34

———. *The Outlook for Rural Youth.* Washington: U S Ag Ext Service Cir 223 S '35. Mimeo. Cooperative Extension Work in Agriculture and Home Economics

———. *Population and Occupational Shifts.* Washington: Bur Ag Econ, U S Dept Ag. Address, Am Country Life Assn, Nov. 17, and Land Grant College Assn N 19 '34

———. "Rural-Urban Migration and the National Welfare." *Ann Assn Am Geographers* 23:59-129 Je '33

BAKER, O. E. and MANNY, T. B. *Population Trends and the National Welfare: Facts and Observations as to Rural-Urban Migration.* Washington: Bur Ag Econ, U S Dept Ag. Mimeo.

BAKKUM, GLENN A. and MELVIN, BRUCE L. *Social Relationships of Slaterville Springs-Brooktondale Area, Tompkins County, New York.* Ithaca: Cornell Ag Exp Bul 501 Mr '30

BEAN, L. H. "Farm Income, Business Activity, and Population Movement." *Ag Situation* 13:20-23 My '29

BECK, P. G. *Recent Trends in the Rural Population of Ohio.* Wooster: Ohio Ag Exp Bul 533 My '34

BECK, P. G. and FORSTER, M. C. *Six Rural Problem Areas—Relief, Resources, Rehabilitation.* Washington: Federal Emergency Relief Administration Research Monograph No. 1 '35

BISHOP, WARREN. "Putting City Workers Back on the Farm." *Nation's Business* 21:16-17 N '33

BORSODI, RALPH. *The Flight from the City.* New York: Harper '33

BOWMAN, ISAIAH. *The Pioneer Fringe.* New York: American Geographical Society '31 (Special publication, No. 13) Part 1: Generalities. Part 2: Chapter 8, Western Zones of Experimentation in the United States

BREITHAUPT, L. R. and HOFFMAN, C. S. *Preliminary Information concerning Immigration into Rural Districts in Oregon, January 1933 to June 1935.* Corvallis: Ore Ag Exp Cir 157 '36

BRUNNER, E. DE S. and KOLB, J. H. *Rural Social Trends.* New York: McGraw-Hill '33 Chapter 1, pp. 1-36

BRUNNER, E. DE S. and LORGE, IRVING. *Rural Trends in the Depression Years.* New York: Columbia Univ Press '37

BURT, HENRY J. *The Population of Missouri: A General Survey of Its Sources, Changes and Present Composition.* Columbia: Missouri Ag Exp Res Bul 188 '33

CARPENTER, NILES. *Immigrants and Their Children, 1920. A Study Based on Census Statistics Relative to the Foreign-Born and the Native White of Foreign or Mixed Parentage.* Washington: Government Printing Office '27. U S Bur Census Monograph vii

————. "Migration between City and Country in the Buffalo Metropolitan Area." In: Himes, Norman E., Ed., *Economics, Sociology and the Modern World. Essays in Honor of Thomas Nixon Carver.* Cambridge: Harvard Univ Press '35 Pp. 269-91

CARPENTER, NILES and HAENSZEL, W. M. "Migratoriness and Criminality in Buffalo." *Social Forces* 9:254-55 D '30

CLARK, CARROLL D. and ROBERTS, ROY L. *People of Kansas: A Demographic and Sociological Study.* Topeka: Kansas State Planning Board '36. Chapter 6, pp. 62-73; Chapter 7, pp. 74-90

————. "Some Demographic Characteristics of the Population of Kansas." *Sw Social Sci Q* 16:11-28 S '35

CLOUGH, WILSON O. "Wyoming and Westward Movement, Natal Statistics at the University of Wyoming." *Am J Soc* 35:808-15 Mr '30

COOK, R. C. "Population Trends in Vermont." *J Heredity* 23:131-34 Mr '32

Corbally, John E. "Measures of Intra-Urban Mobility." *Sociol & Social Res* 14:547-52 S-Ag '29-'30

"The Cost of Drift." *Family* 13:204-6 O '32

COYLE, DAVID CUSHMAN. "Decentralize Industry." *Va Q R* 11:321-38 Jl '35

CREAMER, DANIEL B. *Is Industry Decentralizing?* Philadelphia: Univ of Pennsylvania Press. '35

DODGE, STANLEY D. "A Study of Population Regions in New England on a New Basis." *Ann Assoc Am Geographers* 25:197-210 D '35

DOLCH, E. W. "Geographical and Occupational Distribution of Graduates of a Rural High School." *Sch R* 33:413-21 Je '25

DONALD, HENDERSON H. "The Negro Migration of 1916-1918." *J Negro History* 6:—. No. 4 O '21

Douglass, H. Paul. *The Little Town.* New York: Macmillan. '27

————. *The Suburban Trend.* New York: Century. '25

DUNCAN, O. D. *Population Trends in Oklahoma.* Stillwater: State College of Agriculture and Mechanical Arts. Ag Exp Bul 224 '35

————. "Social Aspects of Rural Shifts of Farm Population in Oklahoma." *Cur Farm Economics* 9:88-93. Okla Ag Exp Bul. Ag '36

DUTCHER, DEAN. *The Negro in Modern Industrial Society: An Analysis of Changes in the Occupations of Negro Workers, 1910-1920.* Lancaster, Pa.: Science Press. '30

Eugenics Survey of Vermont: *Selective Migration from Three Rural Vermont Towns and Its Significance.* Burlington: Eugenics Survey of Vermont. S '31

Florida. Commissioner of Agriculture: *Sixth Census of the State of Florida, 1935.* Tallahassee: State Dept Ag, n. d.

Florida. Transient Coordinating Committee: *Report to the Governor on Recommendations for Federal Legislation, February 1936.* Jacksonville: the Committee. '36

GALPIN, C. J. *Analysis of Population to and from Farms.* Washington: Bur Ag Econ, U S Dept Ag O '27. Mimeo.

————. "Farm Population Starts Gaining." *Ag Situation* 15:2-4 Mr '31

————. "The Trend of Farm Population." *Rural Am* 8:5-6 Je '30

GALPIN, C. J. and MANNY, T. B. *Interstate Migrations among the Native White Population as Indicated by Differences between State of Birth and State of Residence.* Washington: Bur Ag Econ, U S Dept Ag O '34

GAREY, L. F. "Stranded Farmers in Urban Centers." *Social Forces* 14:388-94 Mr '36

GARNETT, WILLIAM E. *A Social Study of the Blacksburg Community.* Blacksburg: Virginia Polytechnic Institute. Va Ag Exp Bul 299 '35

GARVER, FREDERIC, BODDY, FRANCIS M., and NIXON, ALVAR J. *The Location of Manufactures in the United States, 1899-1929.* Minneapolis: Univ of Minnesota Press. '33. Bulletins of the Employment Stabilization Research Institute, Vol 2

GATES, PAUL W. *The Illinois Central Railroad and Its Colonization Work.* Cambridge: Harvard Univ Press. '34

GEE, WILSON. *The Qualitative Nature of Rural Depopulation in Santuc Township, South Carolina, 1900-1930.* Clemson College: S C Ag Exp Bul 287 Ja '33

————. "A Qualitative Study of Rural Depopulation in a Single Township." *Am J Soc* 39:210-21 S '33

————. "Rural Population Research in Relation to Land Utilization." *Social Forces* 12:355-59 Mr '34

GEE, WILSON and CORSON, JOHN J. III. *Rural Depopulation in Certain Tidewater and Piedmont Areas of Virginia.* Univ. of Virginia: The

Institute for Research in the Social Sciences. Institute Monograph No. 3 '29

GEE, WILSON and RUNK, DEWEES. "Qualitative Selection in Cityward Migration." *Am J Soc* 37:254-65 S '31

GILLETTE, J. M. "Urban Influence and Selection." *Am Sociol Soc Publications* 23:1-14 '29

GOLDTHWAIT, J. W. "A Town That Has Gone Down Hill." *Geog R* 17:527-52 O '27

GOODRICH, CARTER and others. *Migration and Economic Opportunity.* Philadelphia: Univ of Pennsylvania Press. '36

GOODRICH, CARTER, ALLIN, BUSHROD W. and HAYES, MARION. *Migration and Planes of Living, 1920-1934.* Philadelphia: Univ of Pennsylvania Press. '35

GOODRICH, CARTER and DAVISON, SOL. "The Wage-Earner in the Westward Movement, I." *Pol Sci Q* 50:1-185 Je '35

———. "The Wage-Earner in the Westward Movement, II." *Pol Sci Q* 51:61-116 Mr '36

GREEN, HOWARD WHIPPLE. *Movement of Families Within the Cleveland Metropolitan District, 1933.* Cleveland: Real Property Inventory of Metropolitan Cleveland. Report No. 3. '33

———. *Movement of Families Within the Cleveland Metropolitan District, 1934.* Cleveland: Real Property Inventory of Metropolitan Cleveland. Report No. 5. '34

GROVES, ERNEST H. "Psychic Causes of Rural Migration." *Am J Soc* 21:623-27 Mr '16

GWIN, J. B. "Subsistence Homesteads." *Social Forces* 12:522-25 My '34

HAMILTON, C. HORACE. "The Annual Rate of Departure of Rural Youths from Their Parental Homes." *Rural Sociol* 1:164-79 Je '36

———. *Rural-Urban Migration in North Carolina, 1920-1930.* Raleigh: N C Ag Exp Bul 295 F '34

———. "Rural-Urban Migration in the Tennessee Valley Between 1920 and 1930." *Social Forces* 13:57-64 O '34

———. "The Status and Future of Farm Tenantry in the South." *Commercial Fert, 1936 Year Book*

HAMLIN, H. M. "Residences in 1932 of Iowa High School Graduates, 1921 to 1925." *J Ed Res* 24:524-28 Mr '34

HART, HORNELL N. *Selective Migration as a Factor in Child Welfare in the United States, with Special References to Iowa.* Iowa City: Univ of Iowa Studies in Child Welfare, Vol. 1, First Series S '21

HARTMAN, W. A. and WOOTEN, H. H. *Georgia Land Use Problems.* Experiment: Ga Ag Exp Bul 191. '35

HASSE, ADELAIDE R., comp. *Social Recovery Plan, Shifting of Industry and Population Groups: A Tentative List of References.* Washington: Federal Emergency Relief Administration Library. 3 parts. '34

HILL, GEORGE W. *Rural Migration and Farm Abandonment.* Washington: Federal Emergency Relief Administration Division of Research, Statistics, and Finance. '35

HILL, T. ARNOLD. "Migration Again." *Opportunity* 10:255 Ag '32

HOAG, EMILY F. *The National Influence of a Single Farm Community: A Study of the Flow into National Life of Migration from the Farm.* Washington: Government Printing Office. U S Ag Bul 984 '21

HOLMES, SAMUEL J. "The Effect of Migration on the Natural Increase of the Negro." In: *International Congress of Eugenics,* 3rd, New York, 1932. *A Decade of Progress in Eugenics.* Baltimore: Williams and Wilkins. '34. Pp. 119-23

HOOVER, E. M. "The Location of the Shoe Industry in the United States." *Q J Econ* 47:254-76 F '33

HYPES, J. L. *Population Mobility in Rural Connecticut.* Storrs: Conn Ag Exp Bul 196 Ag '34

HYPES, J. L., RAPPORT, VICTOR A., and KENNEDY, EILEEN M. *Connecticut Rural Youth and Farming Occupations.* Storrs: Ag Exp Bul 182 N '32

INESON, F. A. *Population Stabilization and Social Relief.* Washington: U S Forest Service. '35

JENKINS, R. L. "Measurement of Attraction of Communities." *J Abnorm & Social Psychol* 28:123-35 Jl-S '33

JEROME, HARRY. *Migration and Business Cycles.* New York: National Bureau of Economic Research Inc. '26

JOY, ARYNESS. "Note on the Changes of Residence of Families of American Business and Professional Men." *Am J Soc* 33:614-21 Ja '28

KELLEY, FREDERICK J. and PATTERSON, BETTY A. *Residence and Migration of College Students.* Washington: Government Printing Office. Pamphlet No. 48 '34

KENNEDY, LOUISE VENABLE, *The Negro Peasant Turns Cityward: Effects of Recent Migrations to Northern Cities.* New York: Columbia Univ Press '30. Columbia University Studies in History, Economics, and Public Law, No. 329

KIRKPATRICK, E. L. and BOYNTON, AGNES M. *Wisconsin's Human and*

Physical Resources: A Graphic Presentation of Conditions Affecting Rural Rehabilitation. Madison: Research Section, Resettlement Administration, Region II. Jl '36

KISER, CLYDE V. *Sea Island to City.* New York: Columbia Univ Press. '32. Columbia University Studies in History, Economics, and Public Law, No. 368

KLINEBERG, OTTO. *Negro Intelligence and Selective Migration.* New York: Columbia Univ Press '35

KRAENZEL, CARL F. *Countrywide Movement of Population in Wisconsin, January 1, 1930 to October 1, 1934.* Madison: Univ of Wisconsin '35 PhD Thesis

KROUT, MAURICE H. "Race and Culture: A Study in Mobility, Segregation, and Selection." *Am J Soc* 37:175-89 S '31

LA FOLLETTE, ROBERT. "Interstate Migration and Indiana Culture." *Mississippi Valley Hist R* 16:347-58 D '29

LAMSON, GENEVIEVE. *A Study of Agricultural Population in Selected Vermont Towns.* Committee on the Human Factor of the Vermont Commission on Country Life. '31

"Land Settlement for Unemployed: Migration to and from Farms in 1931." *Monthly Labor R* 35:512-13 S '32

LANDIS, PAUL H. *Rural Population Trends in Washington.* Pullman: Wash Ag Exp Bul 333 Jl '36

LEECH, DON L. "The Geographical Distribution of High School Graduates." *Sch R* 40:51-4 Ja '32

LEPPARD, HENRY M. "The Settlement of the Peace River Country." *Geog R* 25:62-78 Ja '35

LETT, HAROLD A. "Migration Difficulties in Michigan." *So Workm* 56:231-36 '27

LEWIS, EDWARD E. "Economic Factors in Negro Migration." *Am Statis Assn J* 27:45-53 Mr '32

————. *The Mobility of the Negro: A Study in the American Labor Supply.* New York: Columbia Univ Press '31. Columbia University Studies in History, Economics, and Public Law, No. 342

————. "Recent Farm-Ownership Changes in the Cotton Belt and Their Significance for Migration." *Social Forces* 13:238-44 D '34

————. "The Southern Negro and the American Labor Supply." *Pol Sci Q* 48:172-83 Je '33

LIND, ANDREW W. *A Study of Mobility of Population in Seattle.* Seattle: Univ of Washington Publications in the Social Sciences, Vol 3 O '25. Pp. 1-64

LIVELY, C. E. *Family Living Expenditures on Ohio Farms.* Wooster: Ohio Ag Exp Bul 468 N '30

————. *Length of Residence of the Heads of Families in Selected Rural Areas of Ohio.* Columbus: State College of Agriculture '35

————. "Origin of the Rural Population of Ohio." *Ohio Ag Exp Bi-monthly Bul* Vol 21, No. 179 Mr '36

————. "Population Mobility." *Rural Sociol* 1:40-53 Mr '36

————. *Social Aspects of Land Utilization.* Columbus: Ohio Ag Exp '35

————. "Spatial Mobility of the Rural Population with Respect to Local Areas." *Am J Soc* 43:89-102 Jl '37

LIVELY, C. E. and BECK, P. G. *Movement of Open Country Population in Ohio.* Wooster: Ohio Ag Exp Bul 489 S '31

LIVELY, C. E. and FOLSE, C. L. *The Trend of Births, Deaths, Natural Increase, and Migration in the Rural Population.* Columbus: Ohio Ag Exp Bul 87. Mimeo. Ap '36

McCARTY, H. H. *Industrial Migration in the U.S., 1914 to 1927.* Iowa City: State University College of Commerce, Bureau of Business Research. Iowa Studies in Business No. 7 '30

McCORMICK, THOMAS C. "Urban Migration and Educational Selection —Arkansas Data." *Am J Soc* 39:355-59 N '33

McFALL, ROBERT J. "Urban Decentralization." In: *Economic Essays in Honor of Wesley Clair Mitchell.* New York: Columbia Univ Press '35

McGARRY, E. D. *Population Shifts in Buffalo, 1920-1930.* Buffalo: Univ of Buffalo, Bur of Bus & Soc Res. State Survey Sup 10 '35

McMILLAN, ROBERT T. "Some Observations on Oklahoma Population Movements Since 1930." *Rural Sociol* 1:332-43 S '36

MALIN, J. C. "The Turnover of Farm Population in Kansas." *Kan Hist Q* 4:339-72 N '35

MELVIN, BRUCE L. "Rural Life." *Am J Soc* 37:937-41 My '32

————. *Rural Population of New York.* Ithaca: Cornell Ag Exp Memoir 116 Je '28

Middle West Utilities Company. *America's New Frontier.* Chicago: Middle West Utilities Company '29

"Migration to and from Farms in 1931." *Monthly Labor R* 35:512-13 S '32

MITCHELL, W. N. and JUCIUS, M. J. "Industrial Districts of the Chicago Region and Their Influence on Plant Location." *J Bus Univ of Chicago:* 6:139-56 Ap '33

MOORE, H. E. and LLOYD, O. G. *The Back-to-the-Land Movement in Southern Indiana.* Lafayette: Purdue University. Ind Ag Exp Bul 409 '36

MOSELL, SADIE P. "The Standard of Living among 100 Negro Migrant Families in Philadelphia." *Ann Am Acad* 98:173-218 '21

MOWRER, ERNEST R. "Family Disorganization and Mobility." *Am Sociol Soc Publicaions* 23:134-45 '29

MURCHIE, R. W. *Land Settlement as a Relief Measure.* Minneapolis: Univ of Minnesota Press. '33

MURPHY, PRENTICE. "America on the March." *Survey G* 22:147-50; 180-83; 185 Mr '33

New York State Planning Board. *Rural-Urban Movement in New York State.* Albany: State Planning Board Bul 17 '34

New York State Planning Board, Committee on Social Trends. *A Survey of Social Trends within the State of New York.* Albany: State Planning Board Bul 19, '35 Chapter III, *Spatial Distribution of Population Within New York State*

"Number of Persons Employed per Farm in the United States, January 1929 to June 1935." *Monthly Labor R* 41:358-59 Ag '35

NYLANDER, TOWNE. "Wandering Youth." *Sociol & Social Res* 17:560-68 Jl-Ag '33

OYLER, MERTON. *Cost of Living and Population Trends in Laurel County, Kentucky.* Lexington: Univ of Kentucky. Ky Ag Exp Bul 301 '30

Population Redistribution. Washington: Population Assn of America, Round Table May 3, 1935, Social Planning, Hotel Willard, Washington '35

POTTER, ELLEN C. "Mustering Out the Migrants." *Survey* 69: 411-12 D '33

———. "The Problem of the Transient." *Ann Am Acad* N '34

President's Conference on Home Building and Home Ownership, Washington, D.C., 1931: *Slums, Large-Scale Housing and Decentralization.* Washington, D.C.: President's Conference on Home Building and Home Ownership '32

PUNKE, HAROLD H. "Distribution and Migration of Persons Listed in 'Who's Who,' as Compared with the General Population." *Social Forces* 14:73-80 O '35

———. "Educational Implications of a Mobile Population." *El School J* 33:517-26 Mr. '33

78 INTERNAL MIGRATION

——. "Migration of High School Graduates." *Sch R* 42: 26-39 Ja '34

——. "Recent Countryward Migration and the Country School." *J Ed Res* 29:599-602 Ap '36

PUSEY, MERLE J. "Shift of Population as Affected by Industry." *Current Hist* 32:112-16 Ap '30

REEVES, F. W. "Rural Educational Problems in Relation to New Trends in Population Distribution." *Social Forces* 14:7-16 O '35

REYNOLDS, R. V. and PIERSON, ALBERT H. "Tracking the Sawmill Westward." *Am For* 31:643-48; 686 N '25

ROSS, FRANK A. and KENNEDY, LOUISE V. *A Bibliography of Negro Migration.* New York: Columbia Univ Press '34

ROSS, FRANK A. and TRUXAL, ANDREW G. "Primary and Secondary Aspects of Interstate Migrations." *Am J Soc* 37:435-44 N '31

ROWELL, EDWARD J. *Drought Refugee and Labor Migration to California in 1936.* Washington: Government Printing Office. '37 U S Bur Labor Statistics, Series No. R 480. From *Monthly Labor R* D '36 (Continuation of article of same name by Paul S. Taylor and Tom Vasey.)

RUTLEDGE, R. M. "The Relation of the Flow of Population to the Problem of Rural and Urban Inequality." *J Farm Econ* 12:427-39 Jl '30

SANDERS, J. T. *The Economic and Social Aspects of Mobility of Oklahoma Farmers.* Stillwater: Okla Ag Exp Bul 195 '29

SANDERSON, DWIGHT. *A Population Study of Three Townships in Cortland County, New York.* Ithaca: N Y Ag Exp Memoir 111 Mr '28

SCHLESINGER, A. M. *The Rise of the City.* New York: Macmillan. '33

SCOTT, E. J. *Negro Migration During the War.* New York: Oxford Univ Press, Am Branch '20 Carnegie Endowment for International Peace, Division of Economics and History. Preliminary Economic Studies of the War No. 16

SMICK, A. A. and YODER, F. R. *A Study of Farm Migration in Selected Communities in the State of Washington.* Pullman: Wash Ag Exp Bul 233 Je '29

SMITH, GUY-HAROLD. "Interstate Migration as Illustrated by Ohio." *Bul Geog Soc of Philadelphia* 27:301-12 O '29

——. "The Population of Wisconsin." *Geog R* 8:402-21 '29

——. "The Settlement and the Distribution of the Population in Wisconsin." *Wis Acad Sci Arts & Lett Trans* 24:53-107 '29

SMITH, T. L. "Population and Land Utilization." *Sw R,* Summer, Pp 392-98 '35

SMITH, T. L., BYRD, M. and SHAFER, K. "Mobility of Population in Assumption and Jefferson Davis Parishes, Louisiana." *Sw Social Sci Q* 17:31-7 Je '36

SMITH, T. L. and FRY, MARTHA R. *The Population of a Selected "Cutover" Area in Louisiana.* Baton Rouge: La State Univ Bul 268 '36

South Dakota. Director of State Census. *Fifth Census of the State of South Dakota Taken in the Year 1935.* Pierre, S.D.: State Dept of History, n.d.

SPENGLER, JOSEPH J. "Migration Within the United States." *J Heredity* 27:3-20 Ja '36

STEWART, CHARLES L. "Migration to and from Our Farms." *Ann Am Acad* 117:52-60 Ja '25

———. "Movements to and from Farms." *Ann Am Acad* 142:51-7 Mr '29

STUART, JOHANNES. "Mobility and Delinquency." *Am J Orthopsychiatry* 6:486-93 O '36

SULLENGER, T. EARL. "A Study of Intra-Urban Mobility." *Sociol & Social Res* 17:16-24 S-O '32

TATE, LELAND B. *The Rural Homes of City Workers and the Urban-Rural Migration.* Ithaca: Cornell Ag Exp Bul 595 Ap '34

TAYLOR, PAUL S. "Again the Covered Wagon." *Survey G* 24:348-51; 368 Jl '35

———. "The Migrants and California's Future: The Trek to California and the Trek in California." San Francisco, *Resettlement Administration*, California. '35 Resettlement Administration R9-5-FRS

TAYLOR, PAUL S. and VASEY, TOM. "Contemporary Background of California Farm Labor." *Rural Sociol* 1:401-19 D '36

———. "Drought Refugee and Labor Migration to California, June-December, 1935." *Monthly Labor R* 42:312-18 F '36

THOMPSON, W. S. "Movements of Population." *Am J Soc* 40:713-19 My '35

THORNTHWAITE, C. WARREN. *Internal Migration in the United States.* Philadelphia: Univ of Pennsylvania Press '34

TORBERT, EDWARD N. "The Evolution of Land Utilization in Lebanon." *N H Geog R* 25:209-30 Ap '35

TRUESDELL, L. E. *Farm Population of the United States.* Washington: Government Printing Office. U S Bur of Census, Census Monograph No. 6 '26

TUGWELL, REXFORD G. "National Significance of Recent Trends in Farm Population." *Social Forces* 14:1-7 O '35

TYLOR, W. RUSSELL. "The Exodus from Rural America." *Cur Hist* 35:404-8 D '31

U. S. Bureau of Agricultural Economics. *Farm Population Estimates as of January 19.* Washington. Issued annually. Mimeo.

U. S. Bureau of the Census. *Location of Manufactures, 1899 to 1929: A Study of Tendencies toward Centralization and toward Dispersion of Manufactures in the United States.* Washington: Government Printing Office '33 Prepared by Tracy E. Thompson

————. *United States Census of Agriculture 1935. Reports for States with Statistics for Counties and a Summary for the United States.* Washington: Government Printing Office '36

U. S. Department of Agriculture. *Economic and Social Problems of the Southern Appalachians.* Washington: Government Printing Office. U S Ag Misc Publications No. 205 '35

U. S. Great Plains Committee. *The Future of the Great Plains.* Washington: Government Printing Office '36 Chapter 2, *Population, Settlement, and Land Use*

U. S. National Resources Board. *Report.* Washington: Government Printing Office '34

U. S. National Resources Committee. *The Problems of a Changing Population: Report of the Committee on Population Problems to the National Resources Committee, January 1937.* Washington: Government Printing Office '37

U. S. Public Health Service. *Dust Storms and Their Possible Effect on Health.* Washington: Government Printing Office '35

U. S. Resettlement Administration. "New Settlers Migration to Pacific Northwest." *Land Policy* R 1:1-4 My '35

U. S. Works Progress Administration. *Division of Social Research. Migrant Families, I and II* Washington: Works Progress Administration. Res Bul Nos. TR 10 and 11 '36

VISHER, STEPHEN S. "A Study of the Place of Birth and of the Occupation of Fathers of Subjects of Sketches of 'Who's Who in America.'" *Am J Soc* 30:551-57 Mr '25

WEBB, JOHN N. *Migrant Families (I): Composition, Size, and Employability of Economic Heads.* Washington: Works Progress Administration. Research Bulletin Ja '36

————. *The Migratory-Casual Worker.* Washington: Works Progress Administration. Research Monograph No. 7 '37

————. *The Transient Unemployed*. Washington: Works Progress Administration Research Monograph No. 3 '35

WEBB, JOHN N. and BRYAN, JACK Y. *Migrant Families (II): Age, Sex, Color, Nativity, and Marital Condition*. Washington: Works Progress Administration Ap '36. Mimeo.

WEBB, JOHN N., WESTEFELD, ALBERT, and HUNTINGTON, ALBERT H. JR. *Mobility of Labor in Michigan: a Sample Tabulation of Mobility Data from the Michigan Census of Population and Unemployment, January 14, 1935*. Lansing: State Emergency Welfare Relief Commission. Mimeo. '37.

WHELPTON, P. K. "Extent, Character and Future of the New Landward Movement." *J Farm Econ* 15:57-66 Ja '33

————. "Industrial Development and Population Growth." *Social Forces* 6:458-67; 629-38 Mr-Je '28

WHITLOW, C. M. "The Geographical Distribution of High School Graduates." *Sch R* 39:213-16 Mr '31

WILLIAMS, B. O. *Occupational Mobility among Farmers*. Part 1, *Mobility Patterns*. S C Ag Exp Bul 296 '34

WILLITS, JOSEPH H., Chairman. "Decentralization of Population and Industry." *Am Econ R* 26:171-73, supl Mr '35

WILSON, M. L. "The Place of Subsistence Homesteads in Our National Economy." *J Farm Econ* 16:73-87 Ja '34

WINSTON, S. R. "Migration and Distribution of Negro Leaders in the United States." *Social Forces* 10:243-58 D '31

————. "The Relation of Educational Status to Interstate Mobility." *Social Forces* 8:380-85 Mr '30

WOODSON, C. G. *A Century of Negro Migration*. Washington: Assn for the Study of Negro Life and History '18

WOOFTER, T. J. *Negro Migration*. New York: W. D. Gray '20

YODER, FRED R. and SMICK, A. A. *Migration of Farm Population and Flow of Farm Wealth*. Pullman: Washington State College. Wash Ag Exp Bul 315 '35

YOUNG, C. E. "The Movement of Farm Population: Its Economic Causes and Consequences. In Gee, Wilson, Ed. *The Country Life of the Nation*. Chapel Hill: Univ of North Carolina Press '30

YOUNG, E. C. *The Movement of Farm Population*. Ithaca: Cornell Ag Exp Bul 426 Mr '24

YOUNG, O. E. "Migratory Trends of High School Graduates, 1900-1930." *Phi Delta Kappan* 13:148-51; 159 F '31

ZIMMERMAN, CARLE C. "Selective Rural-Urban Migration." *Am Sociol Soc Publications* 23:104-15. Papers and Proceedings of the Twenty-Third Annual Meeting, American Sociological Society held at Chicago, December 26-29, 1928

————. "The Migration to Towns and Cities (I)." *Am J Soc* 32:450-55 N '26

————. "The Migration to Towns and Cities (II)." *Am J Soc* 33:105-9 Jl '27

ZIMMERMAN, CARLE C., DUNCAN, O. D., and FREY, FRED C. "The Migration to Towns and Cities (III). *Am J Soc* 33:237-41 S '27

ZIMMERMAN, CARLE C. and DUNCAN, O. D. "The Migration to Towns and Cities (IV)." *J Farm Econ* 10:506-15 O '28

ZIMMERMAN, CARLE C. and SMITH, T. L. "The Migration to Towns and Cities (V)." *Am J Soc* 36:41-51 Jl '30

ZIMMERMAN, CARLE C. and CORSON, JOHN JAY III. "The Migration to Towns and Cities (VI)." *Social Forces* 8:402-8 Mr '30

Index

Studies in the Social Aspects of the Depression

AN ARNO PRESS/NEW YORK TIMES COLLECTION

Chapin, F. Stuart and Stuart A. Queen.
Research Memorandum on Social Work in the Depression. 1937.

Collins, Selwyn D. and Clark Tibbitts.
Research Memorandum on Social Aspects of Health in the Depression.
1937.

The Educational Policies Commission.
Research Memorandum on Education in the Depression. 1937.

Kincheloe, Samuel C.
Research Memorandum on Religion in the Depression. 1937.

Sanderson, Dwight.
Research Memorandum on Rural Life in the Depression. 1937.

Sellin, Thorsten.
Research Memorandum on Crime in the Depression. 1937.

Steiner, Jesse F.
Research Memorandum on Recreation in the Depression. 1937.

Stouffer, Samuel A. and Paul F. Lazarsfeld.
Research Memorandum on the Family in the Depression. 1937.

Thompson, Warren S.
Research Memorandum on Internal Migration in the Depression. 1937.

Vaile, Roland S.
**Research Memorandum on Social Aspects of Consumption in the
Depression.** 1937.

Waples, Douglas.
Research Memorandum on Social Aspects of Reading in the Depression.
1937.

White, R. Clyde and Mary K. White.
**Research Memorandum on Social Aspects of Relief Policies in the
Depression.** 1937.

Young, Donald.
Research Memorandum on Minority Peoples in the Depression. 1937.

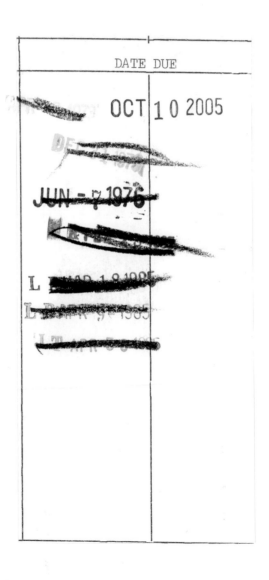